V I N C E N T   O F

A Soldier's Battles in the First Afghan and

Crimean Wars

By G E O F F R E Y   M O O R E

By the same Author:

Kitchener's Pioneers

Three Chose War

Diary of the Doctor's Lady

Just as Good as the Rest

Uniform with this volume

AVAILABLE FROM

Geoffrey Moore, 2 Ivelbury Close, Buckden, Huntingdon PE18 9XE

Price: £2.00   U.S.Dollars 5.

© I.S.B.N. 0 9506360 4 5

VINCENT OF THE 41st

A Soldier's Battles in the First Afghan and Crimean Wars.

By
GEOFFREY MOORE
With a FOREWORD by
Major General F. H. Brooke, C.B., C.B.E., D.S.O.
Last Colonel The Welch Regiment (41st and 69th Foot).

FOREWORD

By Major General F. H. Brooke, C.B., C.B.E., D.S.O.
Last Colonel The Welch Regiment (41st and 69th Foot)

My old Regiment has enjoyed, for many years, what
would nowadays be termed a low profile. Why this should
be is something of a mystery because, in its 250 years
of existence (until amalgamation with the 24th Regiment,
the South Wales Borderers in 1969) it served in nearly
every major war and many smaller, less documented, campaigns;
and from contemporary accounts and official despatches,
it has invariably fought with exemplary spirit and performance.

When I joined the 41st over fifty years ago I very
soon realised the intense, if restrained, pride with which
the achievements of their forebears was cherished by all
ranks. This feeling was intensified when I found I was
expected to teach the history of the Regiment to my platoon,
a firmly enforced tradition. In the course of this I
remember being impressed by two particular points. One
was the continuing excellence of the officer-man relationship,
and the other was the remarkable way in which, on so many
occasions, an NCO or private soldier took command and
continued the fight when all his officers were killed
or disabled.

This last aspect is very well brought out in Major
Moore's account of the services of a private soldier,
Private Thomas Vincent, the subject of this book. After
taking part in the First Afghan War with its appalling
hardships and amazingly long marches, he was with the
41st throughout the Crimean War, the Regiment being among
the first to land, and enduring the miseries of two Russian
winters.

In spite of being wounded at Inkerman (well called
"The Soldiers' Battle") he seems to have remained at duty,
being promoted corporal and later sergeant in 1855. One
may be permitted a wry smile on learning that he had to
relinquish his rank on returning to England in 1856, a
not uncommon reward for military virtue once a war is over!

When the 41st (The Welch Regiment) received new colours
in 1862, there were eleven battle honours on the Regimental
Colour. Private Vincent had contributed to six of them -
Candahar, Ghuznee, Cabool, Alma, Inkerman and Sevastopol.
A proud record, indeed, and I hope the reader will regard
this book, as I do, as a tribute to all the "private men"
who have made the long history of the British Army.

Itchenor
Chichester, Sussex.
22nd August 1979.

C O N T E N T S

ACKNOWLEDGEMENT

To Mrs. Joyce King, Alan Lagden, Esq., Colin Muris, Esq.MA.,FLA and Bedford County Library staff.

BIBLIOGRAPHY

D.A.N.Lomax: History of the Services of 41st (The Welch) Regiment.
Col. H.B.Hanna: The Second Afghan War Vols. I, II, III.
Major A.C.Whitehorne, OBE.: The History of the Welch Regiment.
Lt.Col. Russell Gurney: The History of the Northamptonshire Regiment.

Thomas Vincent of Bath was a smith before his enlistment at Bristol on 19th July, 1839 into Her Majesty's 41st Regiment of Foot. Enlistment, for his part, was for life (this continued until 1847); but it was a somewhat one-sided arrangement since a man could be discharged at any time, usually however on grounds of infirmity through sickness or wounds.

His height at enlistment was 5ft.5.3/8 ins., his complexion fresh, eyes grey and hair dark brown and not so far out from Sir Thomas Gore-Browne's description of the ill-fated young men of the light company who were to suffer grievously in Afghanistan within three years of Vincent's enlistment.

Gore-Browne wrote in his diary, quoted by Lomax:- "When the remnant of the light company came up deficient of many who marched out in the pride of youth and health, I was quite upset, and my voice choked when I tried to speak to them. I had just drafted this company and completed them from the handsomest of the recruits who came with me from Kurrachee (Karachi). Many of them were fair-haired boys of eighteen and nineteen, who had come so lately from England that their brothers and sisters would not have had time to forget them".

Vincent, as we shall see, was in the half battalion of the 41st that fought that day, and survived again and again. He took part in six major actions in Afghanistan between March and September 1842 as well as 20 brushes with the enemy described laconically in his Account Book as "minor affairs in and between the Bolan and Khyber Passes".

It is not known exactly when Vincent reached the 41st in Scinde but he may have arrived by September 1840 or November in time for the move to Karachi from Poona. The first phase of the war against the Afghans was over, but a number of reverses had caused the 41st to be drafted in.

Half the battalion had been sent the 400 miles or so up the Indus to Sukkur proceeding in steamers, the remainder following in river boats. In the Spring of 1841 the battalion was ordered to march to Quetta a distance of nearly 250 miles.

Later in the year the C.O. of the 41st, Col. Richard England, took over command of the troops in Upper Scinde. He was ordered to leave Quetta with only a garrison and the 41st returned to Karachi under the command of Major Gore-Browne as he then was. He reached Karachi on 30th November, 1841.

Then came the disastrous affair at Kabul which General Elphinstone left on 6th January, 1842 with his army of 4,500 soldiers and 12,000 followers in an attempt to reach safety at Jellalabad only 100 miles away.

Dr. William Brydon, alone of that force, actually reached Jellalabad which itself was then besieged.✦ The British presence elsewhere was maintained by General Nott obstinately holding out at Kandahar and by a detached garrison at Khelat-i-Ghilzai, 88 miles north-west of Kandahar, and on the road to Kabul.

Distances to the Army, particularly to the foot soldier were always of the utmost importance. The ground covered on a day's march was invariably recorded and considering the rigours of the climate; one ought to say, the extremes of the climate, and the hardness of the going, this was not greatly surprising.

The purpose of this account is to show how one man marched and fought his way through Afghanistan with the 41st, in a semi-circular sweep entering the country through the Bolan Pass in the south east, proceeding through the central mountainous area to Kabul and out again through Jellalabad.

Vincent's infantry company is not known. He may have been in the Light Company that bore so much of the heat and burden. But the six actions, to which his pay book attests, were the total of the battalion's and he could not have missed a great deal of the "minor affairs" either.

It is probable, therefore, that he suffered neither serious wound nor major sickness to keep him away from the fray.

In the second half of the story, Vincent becomes one of the comparatively few Afghan War veterans to have still been with the 41st when the regiment went to the Crimea. There he was present at the three major actions, Alma, Inkerman and capture of Sebastopol.

In the defence of the Quarries in the summer of 1855, Vincent was noted in his pay book for serving with zeal and distinction which makes it quite surprising not to find him among the lists of those awarded the newly created Distinguished Conduct Medal. He was wounded in the left foot at Inkerman so he may well have been a "survivor" of the hospital at Scutari.

But to return to 1841. At the beginning of the year the 41st found themselves at Sukkur, a well-garrisoned but highly unpopular station on the Indus that marked the beginning of the overland route to Quetta and Kandahar.

At the beginning of February a wing (half the battalion) of the 41st were ordered to Bagh about 50 miles short of the Dadar. However, when they reached Shikarpur, a distance of 20 miles, they were halted for 10 days.

There was bad news from Afghanistan, with serious disturbances at Kandahar and, a new element, a report that the Persians were moving on Herat.

✦ See "Diary of the Doctor's Lady" (Colina Brydon), by Geoffrey Moore.

The wing of the 41st was ordered back to Sukkur and then almost at once, turned round and told to march to Dadar which was reached on March 20th, a distance of 159 miles.

Orders were then received to march to Quetta, a further 88 miles, which was reached after 9 days. May and June brought with them terrible sickness so that the state of the wing became "desperate, the fever-stricken men creeping about like ghosts", Major Gore-Browne noted.

Later in the year, Colonel Richard England, C.O. of the 41st, assumed command of all troops in Upper Scinde and the 41st itself was ordered back to Karachi which was reached at the end of November.

The purpose of including the activities of the regiment in the year before the real action opens, is to show that Pte. Thomas Vincent and his comrades were no strangers to the country and its conditions and had already made some contact with its inhabitants.

It was early in November 1841 that insurrection had broken out, a number of British envoys and officers were massacred and the survivors made their fatal pact with the ruler of Afghanistan, Dost Mahommed, that was to be their downfall.

What happened after the rout of General Elphinstone's army is largely forgotten. It is always remembered that the Indian Government at once despatched a punitive force under General Pollock, which marched through the Khyber, relieved Jellalabad, now under siege, in April and continued on to Kabul.

The part that is forgotten was that Pollock provided only the northern arm of a pincer movement. The southern arm was to be provided by General Nott at Kandahar, relieved and reinforced by a force under England. (Here a digression is necessary for it is hard to decide what rank to give Colonel Richard England at this point. Lomax refers to him as "Brigadier England". However England, himself, signed as "major general" and is so described by the Whitehorne history of the Welch Regiment. It seems reasonable to follow suit).

General England had been at Dadar where the headquarters of the 41st was ordered up to join him. They embarked at Tatta on the Indus, as it happens, on the very day that Brydon made his historic arrival at Jellalabad.

When they reached Sukkur they set off for Dadar with a large amount of treasure required by General Nott. Five companies, in which Vincent was mustered, under the command of Major Gore-Browne left Dadar for Quetta and on the 7th March the force under General England entered the Bolan Pass. Quetta was reached without incident on 16th March.

However, at Quetta there was no forage for the 3,000 camels and the political agent therefore suggested the force should move to Killa Abdulla in the Pishin Valley about five marches on the road to Kandahar. But the whole of the hilly and broken country of the 145 miles separating Quetta and General Nott's force was thought to be held in great strength by forces under Mahommed Sadcekee. It was the third day (March 26th) of this move, however, before the first opposition was met with, when a small body of Afghans was dispersed. The following day the locals assured the political agent that Mahommed Sadcekee had withdrawn from the area. So it was a surprise to General England to find on the 28th that his passage was barred by a strongly held position at Hykulzee. Here, Vincent's paybook discloses, he was to be in a major action for the first time.

The enemy were on two heights, astride the pass. General England ordered the Light Company of the 41st and two sepoy companies to attack the hill on the right, with the remaining four companies of the 41st in support.

Lomax quotes from Sir Thomas Gore-Browne's diary. Who wrote:- "When the convoy closed up, we advanced, and soon discovered the enemy posted on the hills between which we must pass. There appeared to be but few on the left hill, which was by far the highest, but the other was crowded with men and both were crowned with common breastworks".

To understand the action that followed, it must be remembered that the army still carried the Brown Bess musket with an effective range of only some 200 yards. The Afghans were similarly, if as well, armed. Not surprisingly therefore, a major action usually developed into hand-to-hand fighting, especially against as courageous a foe as the Afghan.

Gore-Browne resumes: "Leslie threw a shell on to the left hill which the enemy appeared to dislike; they however rallied immediately and shouted a gallant 'Ullah'. England now ordered a company of sepoys to attack the left hill, and our light company and two companies of sepoys to storm the other in line.

"The 41st was ordered to support them at about one hundred and twenty yards distance. The company on the left failed altogether owing to the steepness of the hill and the strength of the enemy.

"Major Apthorpe took the other three companies up at the double march under a tremendous fire which dropped several on the hill.

"Our light company reached the top and some of the right subdivision got in and were killed in the breastwork, amongst others Colour-Sergeant Sheppard, a gallant soldier and superior man, fell after bayonetting three men.

"The two sepoy companies lagged and never reached the top, which enabled the enemy to concentrate their force on our unfortunate white faces, but sixty-two in number. The result was that they were overpowered and forced back upon us, leaving their captain and seventeen dead and having an equal number severely wounded.

"During this time the 41st were advancing at the quick. I was watching the operation above with the open mouth of anxiety and did not see the enemy's cavalry, who charged from their concealment in good style and at exactly the right time. Eman (Lieut.J. adjutant) rode up and directed my attention to them, and I formed square for their reception. Most of the storming party got into this square, but several were cut up by the cavalry, who came up to our bayonets where many of them were slain.

"One wounded man caught H --(Lieut.G.D.Hutton) by the leg as he was getting into the square. Another came up to it with a dagger only in his hand and there were many instances of like infatuation.

"After repulsing the enemy's horse we were ordered to form line and order arms during which time we had several men wounded. I then formed column of sub-divisions and was going up the hill with the 41st when the Quartermaster General ordered me to form another square. Here we remained for nearly half an hour under a galling fire.

"During this time the four guns were playing on the hill; but being only 6-pounders, the effect was not very great. Several of the followers were wounded amongst the camels, but the enemy made no regular attack on them. At one time a storm of balls whistled between M'Kenzie (Lieut.C.F.) and myself as we were walking on the flank of the square.

"Finding Eman, whom I had sent to ask if I might take the confounded hill with the 41st, did not return, I moved a little further out of fire and found that a retreat had been arranged, the 41st being ordered to protect the guns.

Lomax quotes from two other contemporary accounts. The reveree at Hykulzee thus becomes one of the best documented of all lesser battles.

The first was taken from Colonel Stacey's Narrative of Services in Beloochistan and Afghanistan, 1840-42. Colonel Stacey wrote:

"General England and his staff were dismounted and standing in conversation not far from where the light companies had rallied. I joined them. It was useless to stand and lament over what could not be recalled. A retreat was determined upon. I observed to the general that the day might be retrieved, and offered to lead into the entrenched position with a hundred men, properly supported, and I am confident that I should have succeeded. The men were in courage and anxious to recover the bodies of their comrades. The general replied he had not men. I proposed that the left hill should be attacked first, as it commanded the smaller one.

"The enemy certainly were in strength and very bold, but our men burned with rage at seeing their comrades cut up before their eyes. I think I pressed my offer three times, the last time volunteering to lead with eighty men, but the general felt he had too few and the stake was too great".

The repulse at Hykulzee was described in the Bombay Times, as follows:-

"A detachment, consisting of four light companies from the 41st Regiment and the 21st and 25th Native Infantry, were ordered to charge in line (not in column) up the hill and storm the breastwork on the summit. These amounted in all to one hundred and eighty men. While the remaining portion of the wing of the 41st, two hundred and twenty strong, under cover of four of Captain Leslie's guns, with about seventy men, covered the attack".

From this account and the reference to the strength of the light company, it appears that only 282 men of the 41st were present in this action.

The Bombay Times continues: "The remainder of the force, about six hundred strong, remained in charge of the baggage and were in fact, considering bulkiness, not more than sufficient for its protection.

"Until the head of the storming party reached the crest of the exterior defences, the strength of the enemy was completely concealed from us by their field works, which consisted of a succession of breastworks, improved by a ditch and abattis.

"The ditch is said to have been filled with thorns and the first outwork to have been commanded by a flanking fire. So soon as we got up to them, a dense and determined mass burst out with such fury on our men that, with the advantage of rising ground, of a fire maintained with singular steadiness, precision, and effect from the outer works, and of an overwhelming number in their favour, the contest quickly became so unequal that the storming party were unable to keep their ground.

"Here Captain May of the 41st was shot dead. Sixteen of his men also fell. So soon as they began to retire down the hill, a party of about one hundred cavalry, of four hundred which had just before arrived from Kandahar, and seem, considering their number, on all hands to have been admitted to be the most formidable body of the sort yet seen, dashed round the flank of the hill and burst with the utmost impetuosity on our rear.

"Major Apthorpe of the 20th Native Infantry, who was on foot covering the retreat, was here cut down. His skull was literally laid open. His left arm was nearly severed below the elbow and he was covered with other wounds. A jemadar and two sepoys gallantly brought him off. He lingered till the morning of the 30th.

"The reserve formed square at the bottom of the hill to cover the return and receive the horse. While the storming party, the moment they reached the plain, also formed square about two hundred and fifty yards to the left of the other and there gallantly resisted every attempt to break them.

"The enemy are admitted by everyone to have behaved to admiration. Their plans were ably led and bravely executed. So audacious had they become that many of them were bayonetted close outside the square.

"Some idea may be formed of the obstinacy with which the contest was conducted from the amount of the casualties. Out of four hundred and seventy who were engaged, twenty seven were killed and seventy-one wounded. The enemy's losses are unknown, but must have been severe. They confess to thirty killed and fifty wounded. They fought with all the fury of religious zealots, determined to conquer or to perish.

"The officers admit that a better sustained fire they have rarely seen and that the cavalry as irregulars could hardly be surpassed. The whole affair was one of three minutes. Having found that our squares were not to be broken, the Afghans rapidly retired but in perfect order.

"After having received this partial check and with the difficulty of the ground, the strength of the enemy's position, as well as of his force now developed, it seemed to General England vain to attempt a renewal of the contest. It was therefore resolved to move by the right to the ruined village of Bozar, three miles to the north-east, in which direction the baggage was first ordered to proceed.

"The troops accordingly moved across the plain in echelon of squares, the artillery protecting them by alternate guns and the whole covered by as good a display of cavalry as could under the circumstances be commanded. The whole of this operation was conducted in a manner so steady and soldierlike that the enemy, though closely watching an opportunity of attack, left them wholly unmolested, both during the march and in the position they took up over night.

"A fearful storm of rain and thunder burst out shortly after the troops had taken up their quarters, as if the very elements had combined to warn us back upon our path". It would also have silenced any chatter between Vincent and his comrades for whom with few exceptions it would also have been their first taste of combat.

The following day's march was a most difficult one, says Lomax. It was very ably conducted by General England, but the enemy was on the look out for an opportunity to attack, but were entirely baffled by his skilful arrangements. The troops marched that day from before dawn until after dark. What terrible suffering that must have meant for Major Apthorpe and other mortally or severely wounded from Hykulzee.

A further march throughout the 30th and on the 31st, when the column came under sharp fire from flanking heights. The grenadier company of the 41st under Lieut. Butler was despatched to clear the Kakrese from their position and did so with the bayonet, handling the enemy very severely. After this lesson, the Afghans scarcely troubled the column further and at sunset Quetta was reached. Here they were to wait for the other wing of the 41st and whatever additional reinforcements accompanied it.

The arrival was witnessed by a good friend of the 41st, Padre I.N.Allen who, the following year, published his "Diary of a march through Scinde and Afghanistan".

He wrote: "Thus we were agitated between hope and fear, till on the morning of the 31st I heard they were in sight. I got my horse saddled, galloped to the town, and ascended the citadel.

"Here I found several officers with glasses and, ere long, saw them coming through the pass about three miles distant; the horse artillery first; then the 6th Regiment Native Infantry, then the baggage and followers. Her Majesty's 41st was bringing up the rear and was not yet in sight. They appeared in very good order, but both horses and men very much fagged.

"Seeing some of my friends, I hastened down, and rode out to meet them and learn authentic particulars. At the foot of the citadel I met the surgeon of the artillery, so unshorn and disfigured by the effects of sun and dust that I did not recognise him till after he had spoken.

"Next I fell in with the adjutant-general, all purple, with face swollen and lips cracked from the same cause. Then an officer of the grenadier company of the 41st informed me that they had had a last brush with the enemy and had killed fifteen just on the other side of the pass."

There seems to have been a battle of wills between Generals Nott, in Kandahar, and England at this stage; though how communications were conveyed between them was unclear to Lomax but Whitehorne quotes an unattributed letter describing the two points of view.

General England had already infuriated Nott, it seems, through failing to get through. Now he was aggravating the position by throwing up fortifications at Quetta while he waited for reinforcements.

General Nott is said to have written "a stinging letter to England telling him that his advance and subsequent retreat to Quetta had done more injury to the Kandahar force than twenty thousand Afghans in the field; that the new fortifications at Quetta requiring a garrison of fifteen hundred men were absolutely useless since the citadel, held by five hundred men, was ample for all purposes of defence. Nott is said to have concluded the letter by saying that he would send out a brigade from Kandahar on April 25th and he expected England to meet him at Chaman (about 70 miles from Quetta) without fail on May 1st".

General England was undoubtedly influenced in his stand by the high degree of sickness among his overcrowded garrison. But he got his reinforcements including the remainder of the 41st and duly set out from Quetta on April 25th. Exactly one month to the day, he was again at the scene of his previous reverse at Hykulzee where the high ground appeared once more to be very strongly held.

Pte. Thomas Vincent's pay book shows that he was present and would take part in his second major action before nightfall.

This time we rely on Padre Allen's description of the battle. "The heights in every direction were crowded with men. Horsemen were galloping to and fro, and a flag was displayed at each end of the low hill which had been the former point of attack.

"In the front was a level plain gradually ascending. On the extreme left were some low hills, increasing in height towards the pass, traversed by ravines and terminating in a bluff point overlooking the pass, and completely commanding all around it.

"The point was covered with the enemy. In advance of it, extending across the plain, were some low hills through which ran the road and upon which horsemen were from time to time riding, now rapidly, now slowly, flourishing their swords and curvetting their horses as if in defiance. On the extreme right were some slight elevations to which the treasure, ammunition and baggage camels were drawn off under the protection of a company of Bengal European foot artillery and two or three companies of native infantry commanded by Major Sotheby.

The British force was divided into three columns each commanded by a major of the 41st. The two spearhead columns were commanded respectively by Majors Simmons and Cochrane each with a wing of the 25th Bombay Native Infantry in support. Major Gore-Browne commanded the reserve.

The attackers moved forward as steadily as if on parade, it was said, shouting loud hurrahs as they went. The Afghans abandoned their positions and fled in all directions being pursued by the 3rd Light Cavalry (Poona Horse) under Captain Delamain.

General England lost no time in sending a despatch to the Assistant Adjutant General, Kandahar, describing himself as "major general commanding Scinde Field Force".

In the evening, the 41st paraded to bury their dead of the month before. Mr. Allen wrote:- "Portions of eighteen bodies had been collected. Many of the skeletons were still tolerably perfect, the skin being dried upon the bones and some were recognised by their comrades from the colour of their hair and other marks and one by a wound received in the Burmese War (1825-6). Captain May was discovered by the profusion of fair hair. I scarcely know any lesson on the frailty of man that has more impressed me than the sight of these poor remains."

So much for the dead. But what of the living? Padre Allen
had described the return of General England's brigade a month before.
Vincent and his comrades would have suffered no whit less. And this
second attempt to reach Kandahar was a month further into the hot weather.
Not only were the soldiers totally unsuitably dressed for the climate,
they also had very hard going over the ground as Colonel H.B.Hanna
vividly describes in his The Second Afghan War.

He wrote of the Pishin valley "a more desolate spot can scarcely
be conceived than this upland valley. Of considerable extent - thirty
miles broad by sixty long - its treeless surface is intersected in all
directions by formidable gullies". Except after the snows have melted
"at all other seasons of the year, main streams and tributaries are
alike empty of water, save for a few standing pools all more or less
impregnated with medicinal salts".

Colonel Hanna also says of the route to Kandahar "a vast, treeless
waste broken, here and there, by fantastic shaped hills of marvellous
hues, their jagged outlines standing out sharply against the cloudless
sky, which constitutes the major portion of the Province of Kandahar."

Ninety-five years later, the author's own regiment, the 48th (1st
Northamptons) fighting in similar country just to the east; and wearing
shirts open at the neck, received the order "shirt tails out" and thus
saved some men from heat-stroke which was a scourge of 1842. +

Following the second action at Hykulzee, General England's force
continued their march to Kandahar the following day (April 29th)
reaching the banks of the Lora River where they camped. On 30th they
reached Killa Abdulla a further 11 miles on. The following day was
Sunday and General England rested the column, but in the afternoon he
received a testy message from Brigadier Wymer who said he was waiting
on the Kandahar side of the Khojak Pass "to co-operate". Maybe Wymer
felt he had a point since General Nott had stated the 1st May was to
see the junction of the two forces. Equally, England may have
deliberately waited a day, not only to give his men and beasts a much
needed rest, but also to show who was commanding the Scinde Field Force.

Indeed the march of the 2nd May stood out as particularly trying.
The column moved off at 3.0 a.m. and had what Lomax calls "a most
arduous and trying march through the Khojak through which the thousands
of camels could only pass in single file. And they were troubled
throughout the day by Afghan sharpshooters. The rear guard was on the
march for 20 hours before reaching the camp established by Wymer's
brigade.

+ See "Just as Good as the Rest" by Geoffrey Moore. The 1/Northamptons
  in Waziristan 1936-37.

Even Brigadier Wymer does not seem to have objected to a further day's rest on May 3rd. On the night of the 4th the combined force covered 25 miles to Kolgie and the remaining 43½ miles to Kandahar were covered between then and May 10th. History does not record the reception General England got from General Nott, but he was ordered to camp outside the town near the Kabul gate. However Nott was a Welshman and mutual respect and affection was to develop between the General and the Regiment. Shortly afterwards the 41st were moved into the town so tempers may have cooled.

On the 19th, Brigadier Wymer was sent to relieve Khelat-i-Ghilzai, leaving only a weak garrison at Kandahar of which the 41st formed part.

On May 29th Vincent's pay book records his third major action. On this day Prince Sufter Jung with an army of 8,000 Afghans occupied the heights above Kandahar. General Nott ordered out the 41st, 42nd Bengal Infantry and the 43rd Native Infantry with 12 6-pounders.

The light companies of the three regiments (a force identical to that which was repulsed on March 28th at Hykulzee) stormed the enemy positions and carried them brilliantly. The 41st's casualties were only eleven men wounded.

General Nott tells the story in his despatch. He wrote:-

"The Ghazees (religious fanatics) had about eight thousand men in position and two thousand men guarding the Babawullee Pass and roads leading to their camp. Our troops carried all their positions in gallant style and drove them in confusion, with great loss, across the Urghundab River".

The result of this action was that Prince Sufter Jung surrendered to General Nott and the opposition collapsed in Kandahar Province.

The next two months were spent quietly, if monotonously, at Kandahar while everyone waited for the Government of India to decide on the next move for the forces under both Gens. Pollock and Nott. But Kandahar was no bed of roses. Sir Thomas Gore-Browne notes in his diary that no less than 1,320 men were required for guard duties each day and a bottle of beer, when you were off duty, cost six shillings.

British morale on the whole was low, in spite of the recent success, because of the numerous disasters inflicted by the Afghans and at the thought of the fate of the captives at Kabul taken from Gen. Elphinstone's force in January.

Lomax claims, and he may have been right, that the troops at Kandahar that summer were rearing to go and he writes:- "Judge, therefore, of the delight and astonishment of General Nott's army when it became known that orders had been received for his force to proceed to Kabul".

And the interesting point is that General Nott set off for Kabul from Kandahar on the same day of the year, (August 9th) as Roberts was to march off in the opposite direction to cover the 310 miles that lay between the two towns, 38 years later.

The significance of this is that the climate for the two marches, the one immortal the other almost forgotten, was much the same.   Roberts took less time - but then speed was of the essence with his operation. Furthermore, he was given extraordinary assistance.   For example, as Col. H.B.Hanna points out, Roberts' force had "a searching medical examination to weed out every man who did not come up to a high standard of health.   The transport, 8,255 ponies, mules and donkeys, was chosen with equal care.

Just as Rorke's Drift, the year previously, had been eulogised perhaps beyond reason compared with many another minor action;   is it possible that the "Kabul to Kandahar" march, fine feat though it was, did not also suffer from a surfeit of glory?

Roberts had about 10,000 officers and men and 7,800 camp followers. General Nott set out from Kandahar with 7,000 men including the 40th and 41st Regiments and fifteen thousand camp followers.   Thus Roberts managed with less than one camp follower for every beast while Nott, apparently, needed a ratio of two followers per animal.

The march started in extreme heat, temperatures in the tents reaching 116 Fahr.   Shade temperatures between Kandahar and Khelat-i-Ghilzai ranged from 100 - 60 degs.F.   Dust and the marauding tribesmen, out to get any stragglers, were the worst enemy.   The roadway was quite good, though intercepted by streams and nullahs.   Marching was mainly by night or in the cool of the early morning and an average day's march was 10 miles.

There were three days of fighting from August 27th in which Vincent does not seem to have been involved.   There was first an attack on the rearguard, followed by a trap into which the cavalry fell losing seventy casualties and starting with an attack on grass-cutters from a fort. A bloody affair followed involving the 41st light company, to which Vincent presumably did not belong, at that time.

Afghans had emerged from a nearby fort protesting their innocence, but when General Nott ordered the fort to be inspected, there was immediate resistance from it.   Some of our stolen camels were recovered from inside the fort.   There was much hand-to-hand fighting and little quarter was given.   The fort was fired and the Afghans had some 150 men bayonetted or shot.   Our own killed were 37.

The following day, the Afghans were out on the surrounding hills in thousands, but they kept their distance, while our camels were grazed.

It was on the 30th, that Vincent's 4th general action was recorded. Although there was a report that the enemy was to oppose us at three adjacent nullah crossings, nothing came of this.   However the Afghans were found to be occupying, with an estimated 12,000 men, the square fort of Goyain about half a mile from our chosen camp site.

General Nott made dispositions to attack the fort but before this could be pressed home, the enemy was seen massing on hills to the left, from which their guns also fired round shot.   It was then found that further masses of enemy had assembled on our right flank evidently intending to turn that.

General Nott gave the order to advance and deploy with the light companies skirmishing in front. But the Afghans showed no taste for close quarters and contented themselves with a heavy, if largely ineffective, fire. The light companies continued to advance against the retreating Afghans until General Nott ordered a halt and a return to camp. Great quantities of ammunition were captured, together with two guns earlier taken from the Honourable East India Company.

This action took place 38 miles short of Ghuznee and General Nott in his despatch praised: "the behaviour of the troops, both European and native, was such as I anticipated, and afforded me complete satisfaction".

Curiously he failed to list the 41st as being present. Was he still showing rancour? Padre Allen was disgusted and noted in his diary: "It is much regretted that no allusion was made even to the presence of H.M. 41st Regt., though it had an equal share in the affair with all the other infantry corps present".

Six days later, the army reached the outskirts of Ghuznee, the capture of which was part of General Nott's task. The town appeared to be held in strength and the enemy audacious. The light companies of the 40th and 41st were ordered out with guns to engage them. The firing became very sharp and both regiments were ordered out in support. Pte. Thomas Vincent was on his feet and with his regiment for this his fifth general action.

Padre Allen was, as usual, in a good position to observe the scene. He wrote: "I was in a small garden, in full view of the whole, and with a very good glass. It was admirable to see the light companies ascend the heights; but, poor fellows, they were exposed to a very heavy fire in return for what they gave and many were severely wounded, though but two or three were killed. I could see by my glass the enemy making strenuous efforts to encourage and animate each other."

As at Goyain, however, the Afghans made no attempt to utilise their advantage in numbers and position and they gradually withdrew into the town. Here they had a huge cannon, known as the Zubber Jung (which Lomax interprets as "the heart-smiter" and Whitehorne 'The Mighty in Battle'). Its projectiles, considered enormous, weighed 68 lbs.

The gunnery also was good and the first round pitched among some camels wounding one or two, then the shot bounced over the 41st mess tent and killed another camel. Instant orders were given to shift camp. Easier said than done, however. The move took about three hours during which Zubber Jung fired every 10 to 30 minutes, from which we lost four or five camels though not a man was hit.

Two 9-pounders were then sent to the high ground captured by the light companies and they put a couple of rounds among Zubber Jung's gunners, effectively silencing it.

The following morning, Ghuznee was found to have been abandoned together with a very large quantity of ammunition and grain. During the next two days, its fortifications were blown up and the guns, including Zubber Jung, burst.

The march on Kabul was resumed on September 9th and little of note happened till Sydabad was reached, 24 miles on, on the 12th. Here two men of the 41st were killed by Afghans who found them wandering off, unarmed, in search of loot. But there was little rest as the Afghans kept up a never-ceasing match-lock fire.

A diary published in Colbourne's United Service Magazine and reputed to have been written by an officer of the 41st takes up the story.

The diary says: "The balls from the jingals carried from an immense distance and were most unwelcome visitors. One struck the ground between my tent and Major B's. These balls of iron, about half a lb. weight make a formidable hissing, and are not to be despised. All agree it would be preferable to fight an action every day than to run the risk of being shot in bed each night; and indeed we have had a taste of both alternatives constantly since the 28th ultimo. Altogether the whizzing of balls has become a most familiar sound, but I have no wish to make it my sole music for the future."

The 93 miles (Hanna) separating Ghuznee from Kabul proved the hardest of all because the opposition was increasing all the time. This may have been partly from a greater density of population; a greater fanaticism and desire for revenge as their forts were destroyed.

Or it may have been because the nutcracker movement of Nott's and Pollock's columns were beginning to close and the Kabuli felt themselves about to be trapped.

On the 14th Banee Badam, thirteen miles on, was the objective. Although the country was open and the roads better, the Afghans kept the column under fire from its starting out until late at night. At one stage General Nott sent the hard-pressed light companies of his five battalions to drive the hornets back. This was achieved but at night the sniping continued.

The Colbourne diarist recorded: "A party of officers, sitting late after mess, were disturbed by a jingal ball striking in the doorway of the tent. Many others whizzed by and over". However spirits were high for a letter had arrived from Gen. Pollock telling of the defeat of Akhbar Khan and his intention to enter Kabul the following day.

This he did, on which the diarist remarked: "General Pollock's successful progress and advent this day have saved us doubtless some hot work, but also deprived us of some chances of renown".

In which statement may lie the kernel of the semi-oblivion to which
history has consigned General Nott's feat in contrast to the niche
accorded to Pollock.

On the 17th, General Nott halted four miles short of Kabul to collect
forage for the animals and, there, officers from General Pollock's column
rode in with corroborating detail. General Pollock then took General
Nott's force under his own command. On the 20th the Europeans who had
been prisoners in Afghan hands were brought into camp.

The 41st spent the next 10 days quietly at Kabul and were then
ordered to form part of a punitive force to avenge the murders of Sir
A.Burnes and other British subjects. The objective was the strongly
fortified town of Istaliff, about 37 miles north west of Kabul in the
Kohistan valley. The force consisted of two brigades. The 41st were
again brigaded with the 42nd and 43rd Native Infantry as they had been
at the battle of Kandahar.

III - RETRIBUTION

General McCaskill's force camped five miles from Istaliff,from which
was sent out a reconnaissance in force and this met with sharp firing.
Having completed its task of making a careful inspection of the fortress,
the reconnoitring party withdrew to camp to the great satisfaction of
the Afghans who were thought to have concluded that fear was at the
bottom of it.

They were quickly disillusioned when, at dawn the following morning
the 29th September, the British formed in two brigade columns, moved out
to the attack. Brigadier Stacey's Brigade, including the 41st, was on
the left. This column, covered by the fire of the light companies,
crossed the plain in perfect order and, after passing over some most
difficult ground, stormed the Afghan position with the utmost intrepidity.

The column was led by the 41st Regt. which however arrived in the
town a little after H.M. 9th Regt. (The Royal Norfolk Regt.) which had
carried the ground opposite with the same elan.

Lomax goes on to say that the Afghans, surprised and astonished at
the rapidity of the assault, made for the mountains. However a few
remained to put up a stubborn resistance in some old buildings.

Lieut. William Evans, son of Major General Thomas Evans, was the first to observe the strong point. Gathering some men of his own regiment, the 41st, he led them against the enemy and was shot dead on the spot. The buildings were eventually cleared with artillery assistance.

What came next was hardly to the credit of the British Army, though it was not unique in this campaign of retribution. Istaliff was not only packed with loot seized by the Afghans from the British at Kabul a year before, it was a particularly rich Oriental city in its own right. There was great hatred on both sides and as Lomax records "on the enemy being driven out, the town was given up to plunder and, from all accounts," he says, "there seems to have been terrible licence given to all the troops".

However the men of the 41st and of the 9th did constitute themselves protectors of the women and children. "We are told that", says Lomax "no matter how busy they were looting, at the call of their officers the men of the 41st left their booty and, in small bodies escorted women and children into a place of safety. What is more they rallied a second time for the same purpose. Colbourne's diarist called it "no small proof of manly feeling and good discipline at such a period".

He added: - "though the sepoys were difficult to restrain, unable to comprehend why they should deny themselves full measure of vengeance for their massacred countrymen, whose women were violated and then ripped open, according to the frequent usage among these fierce barbarians".

General McCaskill in a despatch said: "My commendations have been especially earned by Major Gore-Browne and H.M. 41st Regiment for their share in these gallant efforts and for exemplary humanity displayed to the unfortunate families of the vanquished".

The sack of Istaliff continued all day. Jewels and money were not often found; arms, shawls, carpets, emblazoned Korans were the chief spoil. One wonders how much of the plunder was subsequently dumped before India was again reached.

The capture of Istaliff was the last of Vincent's six major engagements in Afghanistan. Though he was to see more of the minor affairs his pay book mentions.

After bivouacking the night in the ruins of Istaliff castle, lit up by the flames of the now burning town, the following morning the pillage and destruction of the hitherto impregnable city was completed.

The following day the column set out to complete its work of destruction. Istalick was burnt and then for two days the deserted town of Charekar was looted of a great amount of spoil, and burnt. This concluded the punitive mission, Lomax hastens to add that there were greater instances of cruelty than this.

On the way back to Kabul another village was destroyed after the piquets had been attacked at night. At Kabul there was a pause till the 11th October, when there seems to have been some eager expectancy of the sack of Kabul.

General Pollock refused to authorise this and contented himself with blowing up the Grand Bazaar where Sir William McNaughten's head had been displayed after his murder prior to the retreat at the beginning of the year.

His troops, both European and native were not however so charitably inclined. Possibly those who had not been to Istaliff felt it was now their turn. They rushed into the town and began a sack compared to which the pillaging of Istaliff had been comparatively child's play.

This is rather borne out by Colbourne's diarist who said that it was men of Pollock's division who provided almost all the European element in the pillaging. It could be said that all that saved Kabul from total destruction was the order to return to India on October 12th.

IV - THE RETURN TO INDIA

The return march set out by the very same route which General Elphinstone's army had used nine months before. General Nott's division in the rear were surprised to see the number of skeletons lying about even within the first nine miles from Kabul.

On the second day, October 14th the Khurd Kabul Pass was entered. Colbourne's diarist describes the scene:- "the sun's rays only shine in this dungeon-like pass for two or three hours at mid-day, and at the early hour of our march through it the cold was intense. Wetted garments were frozen stiff and large icicles pendant on the borders of the stream further attested the severity of the frost.

"A dreary route indeed, but rendered horrid to us by the spectacle of the mouldering remains of our slaughtered fellow soldiers with which it is thickly strewn. Skeleton upon skeleton, they lie in frequent heaps, the parchment-like skin still stretched over the bones, and in every variety of posture, the result of violent and painful death.

"Our blood boiled as we gazed on these ghastly sights and we deemed that little enough had been done in vengeance. Over the next eighty miles of road similar objects awaited us, conjuring up the frightful reality of the scenes enacted when these victims fell; if indeed imagination be equal to the task of picturing them".

So far the Afghans had done nothing to impede the Army's progress. On the 15th, 12.3/4 miles were covered so that Kabul was more than 30 miles behind. Then the Afghans struck, making a desperate onslaught on the 42nd N.I. which was only beaten off with the help of four companies of the 40th and two of the 41st. Our casualties, mostly N.I. were seventy.

On the 16th and 17th the Afghans were busy harassing our rear and trying to get at the baggage. On the 18th Jugdulluck was reached and on the 19th Soorkhab. That day the 41st were rear guard and were on foot from 4.0 a.m. to 8.0 p.m. staving off attacks.

General Nott in his despatches said of this day: "A large body of the enemy attacked my rear guard yesterday, which was under the command of Major Simmons, H.M.41st. The enemy was defeated with considerable loss. I have every reason to be satisfied with the arrangements made by Major Simmons and the conduct of the men under his command."

And so the withdrawal towards the Peshawur plain continued. General Nott's division received constant reminders that they were not the only ones to have a rough passage. As they advanced they came, time and again, upon the corpses of men and beasts of General Pollock's division.

On the 23rd, Nott reached Futtehabad, where the last half dozen of General Elphinstone's army had made their final stand in January, from which Dr. Brydon alone escaped. Two days later Brydon's goal of Jellalabad was reached and the opportunity was taken of blowing it up. Clearly the Afghans made no attempt to defend it.

On the 29th Major Simmons, commanding the rearguard, managed to ambush the plunderers hanging on to his tail. He concealed some cavalry behind a ruined fort and soon the enemy, thinking the rearguard had gone on, debouched onto the plain. The cavalry charged and completely routed the enemy who lost between 150-200 killed.

On 3rd November the Khyber Pass was reached, but the fighting was not over. For that night the Afghans attacked General McCaskill's rearguard from General Pollock's Division, which, as always, preceeded General Nott's. McCaskill's force was roughly handled and lost over a hundred killed and wounded.

This caused Brigadier Stacey, with Nott's leading brigade, to crown the heights until the whole force was safely through the defile. The rear guard, mostly found by the 40th but commanded by Major Gore-Browne of the 41st, had a very bad time and only reached camp after thirty hours continuous marching and fighting. The loss of camels and baggage was immense and would have been greater still but for the excellent work of the rear guard.

There was a halt on the 5th during which Ali Musjid, the scene of one of the major battles in the Second Afghan War (1878) was destroyed.

Colbourne's diarist describes the final scenes. The final day's fighting was on November 6th when the 41st was rear guard. He wrote:- "Having been on rear guard, I saw the last shots fired of the Afghan War and can bear witness that the mountaineers did not fail to endeavour to make the most of their last chance.

"Hardly had the main column quitted the old camp ground, when the piquets posted on the heights hemming it all round, were attacked and a sharp fire commenced.

"At one elevated point, upon which I had my eye at the moment, the Afredees (sic) ascended the opposite side of the hill, charged a piquet from a regiment of the second brigade discharging a volley of stones and then rushing on, sword in hand, with loud cries". This is the first mention of the Afridis joining the Afghans.

"The cross fire of a neighbouring piquet having checked the enemy, they finally retreated altogether on the arrival of a party of the 41st, despatched in all haste to reinforce. Major Gore-Browne commanded the rearguard, of which his regiment formed the chief component, and made excellent dispositions throughout the day."

The Afridis tried the same stone-throwing ruse on a company of the 41st, who turned the tables on them, "and a rush with the bayonet put them to flight with some loss. In the midst of all this, breakfast was going on in the 41st mess tent as individuals could snatch a moment for that purpose", writes the diarist.

"Now a terrific explosion told of the final ruin of Ali Musjid; an enormous mass of earth and stone rose high in the air and fell again with a loud noise, while the smoke and dust enveloped every object around, bright flashes gleaming through the dense cloud ever and anon, as the contest continued beneath its veil.

"At length, the ground being clear, the rearguard commenced its march, drawing in the different piquets in turn, until the column of route was regularly formed on a tolerably open and level part of the road at the summit of a hill and through a narrow pass.

"Owing to a Sikh piquet having prematurely withdrawn from one side of the pass, a part of the 41st with which I was at the time had to run the gauntlet of the enemy's fire in it for a short time.

"Their balls whistled down from the left, while those of our comrades, not many feet above us on the right, sung by close overhead in reply.

"I saw a grenadier hit on this occasion so that he staggered out of the ranks and turned pale and faint with his hand against his side. Being supported for a moment he perfectly recovered and though I had seen and heard the ball strike, not a mark was visible. The buff belt probably saved him an ugly wound to say the least, by causing it to glance off.

"We marched on uninterruptedly from the summit of the hill"(protected by the piquets of the Sikhs and our own troops) "These drew in and closed up as we passed on. An animated and fine scene it was altogether - nothing could exceed the imposing nature of its natural features, such as wild and stupendous mountain ranges afford.

"As in ascending to the summit of this terrific pass, so now
descending to its foot, the road wound along the sides of the mountains
on narrow ledges the rocks afforded, widened and improved to the utmost
that science and skill could accomplish and if the barbarians will but
refrain from injuring it, this road will remain a durable monument,
worthy to mark that the British have been carried beyond these formidable
mountain barriers.

"An attempt had been made to destroy an admirable bridge at one
point, which was more than half accomplished but, as they could not finish
it in time to check our retirement, it is to be hoped that the Afredees
will not trouble themselves about it further, as it is thrown across a
place where the camels of a Khalifa would otherwise find great difficulty
in passing.

"The road emerges into the plains and enters the Sikh territory
through a narrow pass, bounded by towering rocks and here the enemy
occupied two positions on the right, apparently inaccessible and caused
us some loss.   The Sikhs also suffered.   Half a mile further we passed
the Afghan limits and thus ended the campaign and the war."

And so Pte. Thomas Vincent and his comrades had experienced the last
of those 20 minor affairs between the Bolan and the Khyber passes.

The regiment's losses had not really been as severe as one might
expect.   Lomax gives them as one captain and one lieutenant killed and
one hundred and seventeen non-commissioned officers and men killed and
wounded.

Lomax adds that a great number also fell victim to exposure and
fatigue in a country with great extremes of temperature.   Also difficulties
in obtaining transport animals meant that tentage was not always available.

Before they reached the Khyber the 41st heard of the award of a medal
for the campaign.   Authorised by General Order issued in Simla on 4th
October, 1842, there were to be four different strikings.

Major L.L.Gordon in "British Battles and Medals" states that the 41st
were awarded 494 medals with the inscription "Candahar, Ghuznee, Cabul,
1842" in four lines on the reverse.   (The 40th received 669 of this
striking.)

However the 41st also received 105 of the medal with the striking
Ghuznee and Cabul (The 40th had only 3).   This must mean that the 41st
received a draft of reinforcements at Candahar after the battle on May
29th.   The regiment, says Major Gordon, also received 26 (the 40th 64)
with Candahar alone.   These men must have been those who returned with
General England to Quetta when General Nott's division marched for
Ghuznee and Kabul.

Adding the three allocations together this gives an effective strength of 625 so that battle casualties amounted to about 20 per cent of the battalion which, therefore, arrived back in India very much under strength.

Vincent, of course, received the medal with Candahar, Ghuznee and Cabul.   The obverse has the diademed head of Queen Victoria with the legend "Victoria Vindex".   It had a rainbow pattern ribbon watered red yellow and blue and a straight suspender fastened by means of a pin to a steel clip affixed to the piece.   The designer was W.Wyon.

Vincent's medal is not in the Regimental Museum, the Castle Cardiff, nor are its present whereabouts known.

General England was made K.C.B. for his services in the war.   Majors Gore-Browne and Simmons were both made C.B.

As for the rank and file, there were no awards in existence for them at that time and they had to be content with whatever loot they had managed to retain from the sacks of Istaliff and Kabul.

However they were able to share in the knowledge and pride that they had helped to add two Battle Honours those of Candahar 1842, and Ghuznee and Cabool 1842, to those to be borne on the Regimental Colour.

An application from the regiment to add a battle honour for Istaliff was refused.

Apart from his medal, Vincent's only memorial of the war was his pay book, compiled by his officer with some care.   But one can well imagine him standing to attention trying to answer the question "How many minor affairs were you in?"   Vincent was probably lost for an answer.   No doubt his officer then suggested: "About twenty?"   "Sir", would be Vincent's relieved reply at having such a knotty problem solved for him. Had the question been: "About 25?" or "About 15?", Vincent would probably still have used an affirmative, "Sir".

The Afghanistan field force stopped at Peshawar for a well-earned rest before setting off for another footslog.   This time the Punjab was crossed in 36 marches to Ferozepore which was reached on December 23rd, 1842.   This must mean that during the year 1842 the 41st of Foot had covered something approaching 2,000 miles not only on foot but over hilly, stoney and often thoroughly bad going.

Regrettably no quartermaster's returns for that year are known of. The turnover in footwear must have been prodigious.   No doubt, however, each man was his own best cobbler and his ability to keep his footwear intact often was the only thing standing between him and a nasty death. There is a parallel here with the skill acquired by every driver in 8th and 1st Armies in the 1939-45 war, for whom the thought of a broken down vehicle was the perpetual nightmare.

Padre Allen does something to provide us with an answer. Lomax quotes his description of the 41st's entrance into Ferozepore. He says: "They looked most soldierly and servicelike and all the spectators whose sentiments we heard seemed struck with their appearance.

"It was really wonderful that troops - many of whom had been four years in the field, with very scant and irregular supplies from India, on account of the difficulty of carriage, could have had their clothing and accoutrements in such order.

"It is true there was many a patch, and that not always of the proper colour, but there were no rags: and there was throughout a noble and gallant bearing in the men, which far more than made amends for every deficiency in outward decoration."

The Afghanistan field force was seen as a "victorious avenging army" to use Lomax's phrase. As such it was given the most cordial of welcomes. Reviews were held and a grand ball was given in its honour.

The 41st having received orders to proceed to England, embarked in river boats and floated down the Indus to Tatta and was at Hyderabad on February 4th, 1843 when its appearance contributed towards making up the minds of the rulers of that country in signing a peace treaty offered them.

The treaty was soon broken and the 41st were ordered to sieze and occupy the town and fort of Karachi. The trouble subsided and the 41st was ordered to embark for England without further delay. The regiment was embarked in four vessels Rajastan, Neptune, Wild Irish Girl and Margaret. The last of these was shipwrecked off Mauritius and the 9 officers and 216 men of the regiment had a rough time before they eventually reached home in October.

Pte. Thomas Vincent was not, however, one of them. His pay book shows that he landed in England on 3rd July, 1843 and so was aboard one of the three first-named vessels. On disembarkation the regiment marched to Canterbury under Col. England and, with feet soft again after so long at sea, this march may have been as trying as some of those of the previous year.

Since the purpose of this story is to cover the battles and campaigns of one man in two wars separated by more than a decade, it is not the intention to give in great detail the peace activities of the 41st Regiment during that time.

But from Canterbury, the Regiment was ordered in June to occupy much of South Wales where they remained for a year before embarking at Cardiff in June 1845 for Dublin (just in time indeed to witness the beginning of the famine in Ireland that was to drive so many Irish to emigrate). The regiment remained in Ireland until the spring of 1851 when it was divided into depot companies and service companies.

The latter were sent to garrisons in the Ionian Islands, but it is clear from Vincent's pay book that he was not in any of the service companies.

On March 28th, 1853, Lomax records that the Regiment arrived off Malta from Zante.

In the autumn of that year the Regiment was warned for service in the West Indies but the gathering of the storm-clouds between our ally Turkey and Russia resulted in the 41st receiving orders in March 1854 to hold itself in readiness to form part of an expeditionary force to aid Turkey against the Russians.

During the preparations of the next few weeks occurred one outstanding event. This was the issue of 26 Minie rifles to each company and as many men as possible were drilled with them.

The Minie had a rifled barrel and this increased the effective range of the bullet to one thousand yards compared with the two hundred yards of the Brown Bess. It was not yet the day of the breech-loading rifle. That did not arrive until 1869, but the Minie certainly played its part in changing tactics.

On 28th March, 1854 Nos. 5 and 6 Companies, including Thomas Vincent, arrived from Ireland to join the regiment bringing the rank and file to a strength of 850 men. Whitehorne records that the average service of the rank and file was between 5 - 7 years; "a few of the older soldiers had served in the Afghan war."

On the 27th December, 1852, Thomas Vincent had taken himself a wife at Sligo. Her name was Mary. There was one girl born to this marriage.

Facing Sketch Map of Afghanistan.

The distances are those recorded by Col. H.B.Hanna in his
Second Afghan War Volume III.

Sukkur to Jacobadad	45 miles
Jacobadad to Dadar	114 "
Dadar to Quetta	88½ "
Quetta to Killa Abdulla	63 "
Killa Abdulla to Kandahar	91½ "
	402 miles

Kandahar to Khelat-i-Ghilzai	88 miles
Khelat-i-Ghilzai to Ghuznee	137 "
Ghuznee to Kabul	93 "
	318 miles

Kabul to Gandamak	63 miles
Gandamak to Jellalabad	28 "
Jellalabad to Lundi Kotal	52 "
	172 miles

From which figures it will be seen that General Nott's column marching
from Kandahar had nearly twice the distance to cover than had General
Pollock's column from Peshawar before both reached Kabul.

Col. Hanna states: "Afghanistan is a high plateau, intersected by
numerous mountain ranges which are only traversable by narrow dangerous
defiles, or by lofty passes.

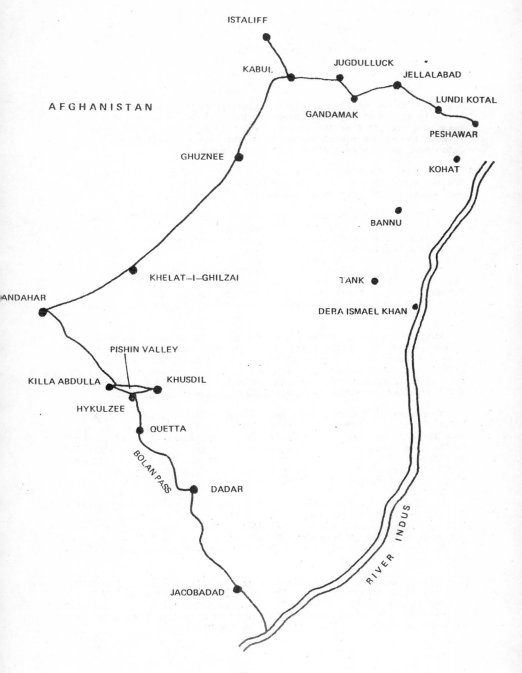

ISTALIFF

KABUL

JUGDULLUCK

JELLALABAD

LUNDI KOTAL

GANDAMAK

PESHAWAR

A F G H A N I S T A N

GHUZNEE

KOHAT

BANNU

KHELAT–I–GHILZAI

TANK

ANDAHAR

DERA ISMAEL KHAN

PISHIN VALLEY

KILLA ABDULLA

KHUSDIL

HYKULZEE

QUETTA

BOLAN PASS

DADAR

R I V E R   I N D U S

JACOBADAD

PART II - THE CRIMEA

V - THE CRIMEA INVADED

The Crimean campaign of 1854-55 usually conjures up visions of hardship due to maladministration and the climate. Generally it is seen as a victory over the Russians which in a limited sense it was, because the allied aim of neutralising the Russian naval base at Sebastopol was achieved after a year of fighting.

The Austrian threat to the Russian flank had already produced the desired withdrawal by the Czar and so the reason why the allies had sent their forces pell-mell to Turkey's side had evaporated.

However, the allied armies were there. The politicians assumed that it would not be easy to reassemble such a show of force again, so for Heavens sake let us put them to some use, seems to have been the prevailing sentiment.

Sebastopol lay near at hand. The Czar does not appear to have expected an invasion in the Crimea. But he got one and Pte. Thomas Vincent, veteran of the 41st Foot was there, in the van, so let us turn again to his pay book to see what he encountered in the year and more ahead.

While there was no Padre Allen present, this time, to chronicle events as they befell the 41st, Lomax has recourse to a number of first-hand sources. Among these were the private letters of Captain (later General Sir) Hugh Rowlands who won the Victorian Cross during the campaign and was later made K.C.B. He had the diary of Captain Edward Lowry and the Regimental Record Book among his primary sources.

To return to Vincent, whose pay book shows that he sailed with the Regiment on April 10th bound for Gallipoli but the transport Himalaya (was the name an omen?) was diverted to Scutari where the 41st landed on the 15th, the first English Regiment to do so. They were quartered in Turkish Barracks. On May 1st they were brigaded with the 47th (The Loyal Regiment (North Lancashire)) and the 49th (The Royal Berkshire Regiment) to form the 2nd Brigade of the 2nd Division.

On June 3rd the 41st moved out into camp near Scutari and equipping with the Minie rifle was completed. Health was good at Scutari but on June 17th the regiment was shipped first to Varna, then it marched to Yuksakova arriving on July 6th and was soon visited by that great scourge of the campaign, Cholera. In common with every regiment there were deaths from the disease.

Whitehorne remarks that there were practically no hospitals and the sick had to be treated in bell tents. Whether Vincent caught the disease is not clear. However he sailed with the regiment for the Crimea on September 5th and disembarked with them on September 14th, 30 miles north of Sebastopol on the west coast of the Crimea.

This landing was entirely unopposed by the Russians with whom we had yet to exchange our first shots. It is curious to note, therefore, that as Major L.L.Gordon records, without comment, that the qualifying period for the Crimea medal, authorised on December 15th, 1854, was back-dated to March 28th of that year. Nor do other authorities attempt to explain this anomoly which surely makes the Crimean medal unique in that it could have been awarded to an individual who left the theatre before hostilities actually began. Regarding the latter end of the qualifying period, more is said later.

But medals would have been the last thing in the minds of the 41st that first night, which Captain Rowlands described in a letter:-
"We landed in the Crimea on the 14th September, without opposition, and had to remain on the shore until four o'clock or more, when we started and marched four miles, arriving on the ground when it was dark.

"Drizzly rain having fallen for the greater part of the morning, we were wet when we got there, and in the middle of the night it came down in torrents. Without fire or anything in the shape of creature comforts we passed a miserable night, lying huddled together in a ploughed field inches deep in mud.

"The following morning luckily was fine and when the sun came round we got all right again. We marched en route for Sebastopol on the 19th at daybreak. The order of march was most beautifully regular."

Those intervening four days had been used to land the artillery and heavy stores. The allies moved off with the Turks and French on the right nearest the sea and the English on the left with the 2nd Division next to the French.

What a grand sight it must have been. The columns were massed together, with bands playing and colours flying. The sun was shining brightly overhead and the heat was great. The troops soon began to feel the suffocating density of their formation and many men dropped in the ranks. Cholera was again evident with its deadly virulence and everyone was suffering from thirst. So much so, that when the River Buljanak was reached after 5 miles or so, men broke ranks to fling themselves down and slake their thirst.

It was not until mid-day that the advance was interrupted by the presence of the enemy. As they appeared in some strength Lord Raglan, the Commander-in-Chief, ordered the Light and 2nd Divisions supported by cavalry and artillery to engage. Thus the first shots were exchanged in the campaign.

But the affair seems to have been more of a skirmish than a battle and did not impede the advance greatly. The troops bivouacked that night without breaking formation and, the following morning, the advance was resumed in complete contrast to that of the day before.

The troops rose in silence, neither drum nor bugle was heard. At 7.0 a.m. they resumed their advance and it soon became apparent that the opposite bank of the River Alma was held in great strength by the enemy.

Subsequently Captain John Edmund Harvey, who was not present that day and received his captaincy on 16th March, 1855 wrote in Vincent's pay book "Present in the Action at Alma 20th September, 1854".

Lord Raglan, who was 66 and had been a desk-bound soldier since Waterloo, naturally adopted tactics that would have been considered appropriate in the days of his youth.

He advanced against the massed Russians in what Lomax describes as "contigious double columns of regiments from the right of brigades, battalions being in quarter columns." This was hardly in keeping with the acquisition of the Minie rifle. As Gurney says in "The History of the Northamptonshire Regiment", "As weapons improved the massed ranks became too vulnerable to exist on the battlefield: the importance of fire increased, and victory was no longer considered to depend necessarily on the charge."

However, there they were, massed in front of the Alma with Vincent among them. A halt was made about one mile short of the river when the enemy opened fire and the whole of the British Army deployed into line. On completion of this movement, says Lomax, the troops advanced to within range of the Russian artillery when the 41st was ordered to advance obliquely to the left.

This movement was performed in open column of sections. The distances were so correctly kept that on wheeling into line again the battalion was in perfect order, although the movement had taken place under heavy fire.

The men moved with the utmost regularity and steadiness, appearing fully aware that their safety depended upon their ready and silent obedience; indeed it was observed at the time that better drilling had never been seen on the regimental parade ground.

Thus Lomax, writing in 1899 captures the prevailing sentiment of the Eastern Campaign as it was called. The 41st, making no use whatever of such cover as the ground might afford, nor opening out to lessen casualties, yet were performing their task with perfect thoroughness.

A second oblique movement was made and the men were ordered to lie down to let the artillery fire over their heads.

Then, to enable our guns to get a better shot at the Russian batteries on the opposite heights, two companies of the 41st were doubled to the rear of the line so that the guns could fire through the resulting gap.

The fire of the enemy was described as "very severe", the ground being ploughed up in all directions by round shot but it was not very deadly. Captain Rowlands observed: "The nearer the Alma was approached, the more plunging was the fire. I believe all our loss was from artillery, and so plunging was the fire that I saw the head of a rear rank man shot off without touching the front rank man".

While the Regiment lay prone, Lord Raglan, with the whole of his staff mounted, passed about thirty yards in the rear of the line of 41st. The group of horsemen were naturally seen by the enemy who opened a much heavier fire. Lord Raglan appeared totally careless of his personal safety in spite of repeated remonstrances from his staff. One can also guess at the comments of the 41st, though doubtless they were made quietly enough to avoid a charge of insubordination.

At length the 41st were ordered to advance, to be halted again just short of the village of Bourliouk, which the Russians had fired. The halts and inactivity and complete silence, except for brief orders to rear rank men to fill spaces in the front rank, never caused the regiment to waver in its perfect discipline. And they had yet to fire a shot.

The Light Division and some of the 2nd Division were now across the Alma. The 41st and 49th with Turner's battery were ordered to move to the right. This necessitated the 41st passing through the burning village, which they did in column of fours. Once clear of the smoke, they were immediately subjected to a very heavy fire of grape. The Alma had now to be crossed. One wing of the regiment crossed without difficulty, the other wing had a considerable scramble before they reassembled in a ravine at foot of the hills held by the Russians.

Both wings climbed the hill, firing on the enemy and forming line. The Light and 1st divisions having stormed the heavy Russian redoubts, the 2nd and 3rd divisions were sent in pursuit of the retreating Russians, keeping up the pursuit for about a mile beyond the battlefield. Three companies of the 41st built and manned a field work covering the right of our position while the remainder of the regiment bivouacked.

Whitehorne lists the casualties of the 41st that day as 4 men killed (Ptes. J.Holmes, M.Hughes, J.Lefevre, S.Putland) and 23 wounded (Sgt.P.Rees, Cpl.D.Jones, Ptes. G.Brown, M.Flannaghan, T.Hannon, G.Cox, J.Pendar, S.Bradley, J.Burtonshall, M.Cullinan, J.Byrnes, J.Johnston, P.Lawler, W.I.Walton, W.Ewins, J.Fowler, D.Jones, A.Kelly, W.Lamb, W.M'Goldrick, J.Kennedy, D.Naughton, J.Skinner.)

The losses of the British Army as a whole were 2002, mainly in storming the heavy redoubts. The following two days were spent in recovering the wounded and in burying the dead. Among the latter were victims of the cholera, including men of the 41st, who died in the night following the battle.

When the allies resumed the advance towards Sebastopol on September 23rd, they found plenty of evidence, in the form of abandoned knapsacks and accoutrements strewing the road, of the panic-stricken flight of the Russians in what had been a decisive defeat.

Sebastopol was first seen during the march, resumed on the 24th, and the accumulation of abandoned equipment actually increased as evidence of the hurried retirement of the enemy, who had not even waited to make a stand.

Lomax describes the bivouac site on the 24th as "a charming and picturesque spot" on the Belbec. As the same time cholera again made itself conspicuously prominent.

What was in progress was a circling movement across the broken and hilly peninsula east of Sebastopol at the end of which lay the squalid hamlet of Balaclava. Once that was seized, as it was on the 26th September, the siege of Sebastopol had begun. It seems unlikely that anyone, then, foresaw that the siege would not be drawn to a successful conclusion until the following September.

Vincent appears to have gone through it all and to have shown a remarkable frugality as well. His pay book reveals, during the years of peace-time soldiering that he regularly had a new coatee, pair of trousers and pair of boots annually. Those issued to him in April 1854 saw him through till January 1855 when he drew a new coatee, trousers and two pairs of boots. He found it necessary to take a third pair in August 1855. The fact that the Quartermaster was able to provide them speaks well for the administration of the regiment at that time. Incidentally in his pay book for 1855 he had inexplicably become William Vincent, an error that stood uncorrected until a later page.

However to get back to the line of march. The 25th was only supposed to be one, short in distance, but as Captain Rowlands observed: "the hardest day we have had, having been fifteen hours on the line of march - most of the time without water".

Yet the distance from their camp site on the Belbec to their objective Mackenzie's Farm, on the road between Baktchi Serai and Sebastopol appears to be only some 5-7 miles as the crow flies.

Against this was the thickness of the undergrowth, through which progress was only possible in single file and the fact that they seemed to have missed their objective, striking the river Tchernaya some five miles further on. They did not turn back since they were now almost in sight of Balaclava and the sea. Both were reached on the following day.

Lomax gives the soldier's personal load during this flank march. It consisted of blanket, greatcoat, pair of boots, shirt, pair of socks, three day's salted rations and ammunition. The officers carried much the same though dispensing with a spare shirt and socks and they carried revolvers against the men's Minies and presumably a sword besides, which must have been a great nuisance at times.

34

Menschikoff, the Russian commander, having brought his shattered
forces back to Sebastopol was, nevertheless determined to move into the
open country to the east of the base and north of Balaclava. He did so
on the 25th moving across the face of the allied army with neither side
aware of the other's existence.   Strange as it may seem that the allies
took no steps to thrust scouts forward, it is even more remarkable that
the Russians, on their own ground, should have been so utterly void of
intelligence.

Sebastopol had not been deserted, however.   Left behind in charge
was Todleben a brilliant engineer, who had command of a garrison of 30,850
men and 5,000 trained workmen.   The town was already surrounded with a
continuous line of stone loop-holed walls and earthwork batteries.   All
non-combattants had been evacuated and to cap it all, this was a base and
a well equipped arsenal from which it must have been a simple matter to
replace the arms and accoutrements so wantonly thrown away in the flight
from the Alma.

The 2nd Division had, by now been reduced to 3,000 effectives of
which the 41st was by far the strongest unit with more than 500 men.
They included the ubiquitous Vincent who was to register his 27th action
against the enemy in the battle of Little Inkerman on October 26th.

This action, though a greater achievement than Balaclava which was
fought on October 25th, has had the historical misfortune of being squeezed
into oblivion by the glamour of the second-best remembered of all 19th
Century land battles.

The Russian objective at Balaclava was to sever our communications
between Balaclava and our positions on what were called the Uplands.   In
spite of the charges of the Heavy and then the Light Brigades and the
"Thin Red Line" stand of the 93rd Highlanders, the Russians succeeded in
their strategic objectives and forced us into a wide diversionary route
and can therefore claim to have gained the day.

But they lost the battle of Little Inkerman which would have earned
the British forces engaged a clasp to the campaign medal in many another
Victorian war, especially in the Second Boer War of 1899-1902.

Vincent's pay book calls it "a sortie".   So it was from the Russian
point of view.   A sortie intended to widen the wedge driven into the
allied line.   It was about 2.0 p.m. when heavy Russian columns crossed
a feature known as Cossack Hill, supported by artillery, and pushed back
the piquets commanded by Major James Eman of the 41st.

But these piquets fought with great obstinacy and delayed the Russian
advance long enough for the whole division to form in line and our own
artillery then opened fire on the advancing masses of Russians with
excellent effect.

The light company and Nos. 5 and 6 companies of the 41st were involved
in supporting the piquets.   Four more companies of the 41st, under Lt.Col.
George Carpenter, then advanced rapidly along a spur held by the enemy and
completely drove them off it.   It was during this advance that the Regiment
gained its first Victoria Cross.

Sgt. Ambrose Madden led a party of his company and cut off some Russians in a quarry. He succeeded in taking an officer and fifteen men prisoner, three of whom he personally and alone captured. For this he was awarded the Victoria Cross, although of course it was not instituted by Queen Victoria until 1856 and Madden's award was not gazetted until February 24th, 1857.

Curiously D.H.Parry in "Britain's Roll of Glory" attributes this action to the Battle of Inkerman on November 5th.

In the affair the 41st lost their first officer, Lieut. Hugh Harriott, who died of wounds and Whitehorne supplies the names of other casualties. Pte. John Martin killed, Pte. Daniel Donovan died of wounds, five men seriously wounded; Robert Dudley, Charles Light, Robert Hanrahan, John Clough and William Tilley and Michael Grace slightly wounded.

The climax was approaching. The Russians were known to have received substantial reinforcements. The French were ready to attack expecting our co-operation, and vigilance on Inkerman Heights was stepped up. Piquets were pushed further forward; night patrolling and reconnaissance were increased and vigilance maintained to guard against a surprise night attack. But the dividional commander Sir de Lacy Evans was far from happy. He wrote in a letter, Whitehorne quotes, at the end of October: "I have but six hundred men on this front position. The troops are completely worn out with fatigue. This is most serious."

We know from his paybook that Vincent was there among the six hundred.

VI - INKERMAN

The Battle of Inkerman has always been known as the "Soldier's Battle", which tends to imply that the generalship was rotten and only the stubborn bravery of the fighting man saved the day.

This tends to give a wrong picture. The fact is that the British, very thin on the ground which allowed for no proper reserves and holding the northern sector astride the road from Tchernaya River to Balaclava, were assailed by two greatly superior Russian Armies whose aim was to make the whole allied position untenable. The Russians failed largely because of the magnificent fighting qualities displayed especially by the 2nd Division. The 41st has every reason to be immensely proud of INKERMAN on its Colours.

The 2nd Division, as has been described, was very much on the alert and, through active patrolling, had a very much better knowledge of the ground over which the battle was fought.

But the exact significance of the continual ringing of church bells
in Sebastopol on the night of the 4th November, a Saturday, and clearly
audible in the 2nd Division camp was not appreciated. As a result,
however, extra vigilance was ordered and a deep personal reconnaissance
was made by an officer of the Loyals, (Lt. the Hon. B.M.Ward), though it
proved negative.

The 2nd Division, at the southern end of Inkerman Ridge which
stretched north of our positions till it overlooked Sebastopol harbour,
was guarding the narrowest part. This was to be the objective of the
converging Russian columns.

The main Russian assault which was not at all co-ordinated with the
secondary force, issued from Sebastopol itself. Under General Soimonoff
it consisted of 19,000 men and 38 guns. Its route was to take it straight
across the front of the British Light Division on Victoria Ridge.

Meanwhile General Pauloff with 16,000 men and 96 guns was to come
from near the mouth of the Tchernaya River where it ran into Sebastopol
harbour. This force was to divide into two, to sweep round both flanks
of Inkerman Ridge. Its objective included an abandoned feature to the
extreme right of 2nd Division's position called the Sandbag Battery.

The weather had an important bearing on the opening of the battle,
since there was a great deal of patchy mist in the valleys which would,
however, lift from time to time, but in general made co-ordination of
the battle, on both sides, more difficult.

Vincent and his comrades were lucky to be under the command of junior
officers of the 41st who were men of outstanding ability. Three of them
were to become Colonels of the Regiment and one, Captain Rowlands, was to
win, that day, the Regiment's second Victoria Cross.

The battle was opened, in fact, by the Grenadier company of the 41st,
53 strong under Captain Rowlands and Lieut. William Allan (Later Major
General). They had relieved the night piquet at 5.0 a.m.

Captain Rowlands described the opening events:- "On the morning of
the 5th, I and the company were for outlying piquet. Colonel Haly of the
47th was Field Officer of the day and he gave me my choice. · I selected
Cossack Hill (alias Funk Point).

"When I passed through the night piquet you cannot imagine a more
cheerless aspect. Day had scarcely commenced breaking in the East, and
a damp cold mist clung to the ground, making objects indistinct or rather
imperceptible at a few yards distance.

"On arriving at Cossack Hill, I halted the company about half way
up and went out to plant sentries 150 yards over the hill. Having done
so, I returned to the company which had just piled arms and ordered the
men to take off packs, when the sentries commenced firing in a most
determined way.

"I ran up to enquire the cause when one shouted out that there were columns of Russians close to them. I stood to my arms and advanced in extended order, thinking it was a sortie something like that of the 26th. On getting to the top of the hill I found myself close upon, very truly, thousands of Russians.

"I immediately gave an order to retire, which was done for about 200 yards, when I halted on the next high bit of ground and lay down quietly waiting for them. Fitzroy (Lieut.G.) who was in support of me then came up with the Light company. His men I likewise extended to reinforce my own.

"When we retired the Russians came on with the most fiendish yells you can imagine. We commenced firing. To my dismay, I found that half the firelocks missed fire, which dispirited the men. At this period the Russian columns opened with their field pieces, pouring in grape and shell.

"We then got some reinforcements of the 55th (The Border Regt.) and the 30th (East Lancashire Regt.) but were gradually obliged to retire. I begged and entreated Colonel Haly to allow me to charge, which he did. After a little hand-to-hand work we turned them and drove them back about 500 yards, when we were met by a fresh column and compelled to retire."

Captain Rowlands did not however mention one incident that took place during the hand-to-hand fighting. Col. Haly was surrounded and dragged from his horse by Russians. Rowlands, seeing the danger, collected a few men and dashed forward to his assistance. After a severe struggle he managed to rescue the Colonel. For this action and his general conduct that day he received the Victoria Cross.

This was gazetted together with that to Sgt. Madden on February 24th, 1857 and referred to "his gallant exertions in holding the ground occupied by his advance piquet against the enemy at the commencement of the Battle of Inkerman".

The heavy firing had aroused the whole of the 2nd Division, says Lomax and the 41st, first to be engaged and numbering 525 men had attacked a column of four thousand Russians.

Major Eman was in command, Lt. Col. Carpenter being the senior field officer of the day. Major Eman led the battalion in line towards the Sandbag battery. It must have been a brave sight. The Colours were carried by Lieut. Armar Lowry and Lieut. John Stirling.

The advance continued until two Russian Regiments, Taroutine and Catherinburg, 4,000 strong and in a solid mass of columns were encountered. These two battalions had been present at the Alma and were in no better mood to stand and fight. The new Minie rifle in the hands of the 41st seems to have behaved itself this time, for Lomax says that the fire was heavy and well directed. Without further ado, the Russian buglers sounded the retire and their columns turned.

The 41st were keen to follow up but soon fell foul of the thick
undergrowth and were checked by General Adams the brigade commander.
However the Sandbag battery was now firmly in our hands. It was
designed for two guns and was almost impossible for infantry to defend
because of its high walls. So the 41st took up lying positions around
it and were joined by three companies of the 49th bringing Gen. Adams'
force up to 700 men. The weather clearing a little revealed that this
small force was opposed by about 10,000 Russians.

General Adams called for assistance from the Duke of Cambridge
commanding the Guards, but without waiting for it, decided that as
action was inevitable, he would attack first.

Accordingly, two companies of the 41st, Nos. 3 and 4 were pushed out
in front to engage the Russian skirmishers who were operating in closer
order than our own men and suffered severely from our own fire, being
gradually thrown into disorder.

The mist had again descended and taking advantage of it, the two
companies charged. Unchecked by the Russian musketry fired into the
mist, and in spite of casualties the two companies pressed on through the
thick brushwood.

But it was as gallant, and as hopeless a charge as that of the Light
Brigade. There was heavy fire from the main body of the Russians,
estimated at 4,000 directly in front, which caused casualties but did
not stop the two companies from getting to hand-to-hand combat with the
bayonet. Three officers of the 41st, Captain Edwin Richards, Lieuts.
John William Swaby and Alfred Taylor were all killed and the survivors
found themselves overwhelmed.

General Adams saw the error into which the skirmishers had fallen
and they were now retiring up the slope in batches, leaving a clear field
of fire for the extended line of the remainder of the force from which
the most destructive fire was poured into the Russians.

Although the Russians returned measure for measure, Lomax comments
that the superior training and rifles of the British began to have effect
and the leading companies of the Okhotsk Regiment were thrown into
disorder. Two more Russian battalions which came to their assistance
were soon in little better state.

However behind these two battalions came a Russian Sapper battalion
and two further infantry battalions, one on each flank advanced on the
small British force like the horns of a Zulu impi. Lomax graphically
described the scene:-

The firing, already heavy, was now redoubled. The dark grey masses
of the Russian battalions moved up the slope as if impelled by force
from behind. Their dead lay in heaps, but ranks were filled up and
nothing seemed capable of stopping their obstinate advance.

"The 41st and 49th, cheered by the voice of their brigadier, fought on in the hope, perhaps, that this attack was going to be as speedily repulsed as that of the 26th October. But they were soon undeceived. Those grim-looking masses were growing nearer and nearer.

"The flanking pressure was speedily making itself felt. The 41st and 49th would not retire and, gradually finding themselves broken up into small parties, doggedly resisted the enemy's advance as best they could.

"Major Eman, finding his men after some moments of fighting getting inextricably confused amongst the brushwood and seeing the danger of being outflanked, ordered the regimental call and the "halt" to be sounded.

"The men hearing their own call immediately took up any little defensive position which offered itself and once more commenced a repetition of that accurate and deadly firing which had so discomfited the Russians in the early stages of the fight.

"The enemy were momentarily checked. But the Russian artillery opened up on the British positions making the slope untenable."

About this time General Adams was wounded in the foot, later dying from the effects of it. All too often in the Crimea, as in the Indian Mutiny (See Diary of the Doctor's Lady) a relatively minor wound ended by proving fatal.

Three of our own field guns under Capt. Hamley were brought up to reply to the Russian artillery and, to give them a clear field of fire, our infantry withdrew to higher ground.

This effectively ended the part played by the 41st as a battalion. On reaching Mount Head it was split up into small parties which became mixed with similar detachments of other regiments.

Meanwhile Gen. Adams' appeal to the Guards for assistance had met with response. Two battalions of Guards had arrived and attacked thirteen Russian battalions who were by now holding the Sandbag battery.

The battle had now turned into one of the most furious conflicts in which the British Army was ever engaged. Sir William Russell, whom Lomax quotes, called it "the bloodiest struggle ever witnessed since war cursed the earth".

The fact is that, by this time, the Russians were refusing to give way in the face of a British bayonet charge. On the contrary they were, according to Russell, mounting many of their own. Much of the fighting in the vicinity of the Sandbag battery was, in fact, with cold steel rather than musketry fire. In fact, there was almost certainly an acute shortage of rifle ammunition by this time. The British Army was obviously too disorganised to have maintained ammunition supplies.

Sgt. Kehir of the 41st was awarded the Distinguished Conduct medal on the recommendation of the 2nd Division's assistant quartermaster general, and his deed may have been typical of so many which went unnoticed. Col. Percy Herbert, the A.Q.M.G. brought Sgt. Kehir to the attention of his commanding officer for "having precipitated himself upon several of the enemy who were attempting to get into the Sandbag battery when there were very few English there, rushing desperately through an embrasure and with his fixed bayonet putting the Russians to flight. He was severely wounded in five places".

Lieut. Henry Bush commanding a few of the 41st took up position behind a low stone wall from where they were long able to harass the enemy before resorting to a charge (lack of ammunition, perhaps, though Lomax does not say).

Major Julius Goodwyn found himself surrounded by Russians but used his new-fangled revolver to such effect that he put them to flight.

Not so fortunate was Lt. Col. George Carpenter, the C.O. As senior field officer of the day, he had been away from the battalion but he rejoined them when they were in front of the Sandbag battery and, almost immediately, was shot through the thigh. He was in the thick of it and surrounded by the enemy, was dragged from his horse. The Russians had already earned an unsavoury reputation for their treatment of wounded and, in Col. Carpenter's case, they added to this reputation.

Although wounded and lying on the ground, he was bayonetted several times. Too late, unfortunately, two soldiers saw his desperate condition. A private of the 55th (The Border Regt.) T. Beach, was the first to come to his assistance. With his fixed bayonet he engaged the Russians, killing two, and was then joined by Pte. Patrick Hurley of the 41st and as Lomax says: "These two gallant men eventually put to flight the perpetrators of a dastardly offence".

Hurley, later a corporal, received the D.C.M. and gratuity, while Beach provided the Border Regt. with one of its two pre-1895 Victoria Crosses.

Colonel Carpenter survived for a short time after the battle and long enough to give evidence of how he had been treated by the Russians. The allies had set up a commission to enquire into the manner in which the Russians had behaved towards our wounded at Inkerman and this was one of the commission's principal cases.

Regrettably, history does not record whether the Czar promised to be a better boy in future or, indeed, took the slightest notice of the commission's findings.

What eventually seems to have decided the "soldiers' battle" was the arrival of French reinforcements under General Bosquet who was clearly amazed to see pockets of men fighting an apparently unco-ordinated battle. Nevertheless the French pitched in, and with all the elan of their race undoubtedly helped to persuade the Russians that the objectives of the day were unlikely to be attained.

Although the Russians did not at once give ground, nevertheless by 10 o'clock they commenced to retire towards Sebastopol and by 2.30 p.m. the heights and slopes of Inkerman were clear of enemy.

The Russians left behind 11,000 dead and dying against a very much smaller number of British casualties. The victor of the day was, Lomax points out, the Minie rifle.

Although the majority of the Russians died from rifle fire, bayonets also took their toll. And here a gruesome comment from Lomax, who says that our men found it very difficult to penetrate the thick greatcoats of the Russians with the bayonet and, towards the end of the battle, nearly always thrust against their adversaries' throats.

The 41st brought their wounded out of action with them as they retired up the slope of the hill. Then came the tally.

Apart from the five officers of the 41st killed and already mentioned, the regiment lost, Whitehorne records, Sgt. Major J.Spence and Sgt.J.White killed together with two corporals and 30 privates. He names these as Cpls. T.Jones and W.Shaughnessy; Ptes. J.Benjamin, P.Brodie, W.Ball, T.Bayford, J.Burnes, W.Bostock, J.Cooper, J.Coghlan, J.Daily, D.Davies, J.Daniels, J.Evans, D.Evans, P.Falsey, W.Finn, T.Keeffe, W.Kennedy, T.Lillis, J.M'Donald, J.Murphy, T.Murphy, P.Meally, M.Moran, P.O'Brien, W.Oliver, M.Phillips, T.Reilly, G.Williams, G. Woods, T.Williams.

The officers wounded were six. They were Captains Henry Meredith, Hugh Rowlands and Frederick Blight; Lieuts. Henry Bush, George Fitzroy and Lt. and Adjutant William Johnston.

The wounded among the rank and file is uncertain. The only one to be absolutely certain about is Private Thomas Vincent who was wounded in the left instep in this battle.

The Regimental Record Book gives the total of rank and file wounded that day as 152. The London Gazette Extraordinary dated 11th December, 1854, containing a revised list of casualties, gives the rank and file wounded at Inkerman and admitted to Scutari hospital as 92 excluding S.M.Spence. Lomax explains the discrepancy as saying that "there were a great number of men who received slight injuries not necessitating their withdrawal from the regiment."

Vincent's wound was of sufficient severity to be noted in his pay book. He may have been unable to make his own way back to our lines and been among the wounded for whom search had to be made through the thick undergrowth.

The Russian Commander-in-Chief was asked for, but declined to give agreement to, a short armistice to enable the dead to be buried and the wounded succoured. This was considered very uncivilised of him and it meant our own weary soldiers doing the job for both sides.

The condition of the 41st after the battle was shown by Regimental
Orders under which the Quartermaster took command of one company, and
the adjutant, in spite of being wounded, took command of two more.
All units of 2nd Division had suffered severely, but piquets were just
as urgently required. The division could not be withdrawn and replaced
by fresh troops. The expedient therefore was found of detailing piquet
duties by number of men instead of by companies.

To add to the misery, the Russian artillery fire had made a shambles
of the 2nd Division's camp and tents were riddled with shot.

On November 14th a very bad hurricane added acutely to the misery
of everyone. Only two of the 41st tents were still standing by 4.0 p.m.
However the men themselves had taken refuge in nearby ravines throughout
the storm.

Nevertheless they had won a notable victory, not least in thwarting
the Russian plans. For the Russians, too, the battle had proved costly
in casualties, which Whitehorne gives as 12,000 including 256 officers.
The total British losses were 39 officers killed and 91 wounded; 558
n.c.o's and men killed and 1669 wounded. The French casualties were
13 officers and 130 men killed; 36 officers and 750 men wounded.

Queen Victoria wrote to Lord Raglan to send her warm acknowledgements
to her troops for their "noble exertions in a conflict which is unsurpassed
in the annals of war for persevering valour and chivalrous devotion.
Let not any Private Soldier believe that his conduct is unheeded. The
Queen thanks him, his country honours him."

Meanwhile practical help was at hand for the 41st in the shape of a
draft from Templemore of 6 ensigns and 100 men. They reached camp in
time to catch the hurricane of the 14th.

Captain Edward Lowry in his diary, quoted by Lomax describes their
arrival. He was one of the six ensigns. He wrote: "... the detachment
landed at Kamiesch on the evening of the 13th and was told to find its
own way as best it could. A tremendous hurricane was blowing. There
was no one to show the way. After proceeding a short way under Ensign
Peddie, who disappeared altogether in the dark, the others halted by
a stone wall for the night. At daylight they went ahead, and reached
their destination at intervals during the next two days."

As there were only 12 officers left with the 41st at that time, the
arrival of six ensigns must have been particularly welcome and 100 men,
too, to spin out the piquet duties.

But it is difficult to know whether to be more sorry for the survivors
of Inkerman or the reinforcements thus rudely jolted into the worst horrors
of war. It was in fact the beginning of the worst winter of campaigning
that the British Army probably ever experienced and that was the foundation
of the dire reputation the Crimean War achieved.

Lomax relies on Sir Edward Hamley's account.   He wrote:-
"With this day (November 14th) began our dire season of calamity.   At
the close of the storm the evening had brought down snow and henceforth
the soil of the devastated camps afforded in no respect better lodging
than the rest of the surrounding wold.

"The sick, the wounded (poor Vincent), and the weary lay down in
mud.   The trenches were often deep in water and when night put an end
to the rifle fire on both sides, the soldiers sat there cramped, with
their backs against the cold, wet, earth.

"A still worse evil was that men seldom pulled off their wet boots,
fearing they might not be able to draw them on again.   Their feet
swelled in them, the circulation was impeded and, on cold nights, frost
bite ensued ending at best in mutilation.

"Coming from the trenches, the men had to go far afield to seek
for roots wherewith to cook their food.   It is hardly surprising that
many preferred to employ their short intermissions of duty in such repose
as was obtainable and ate their salt pork uncooked.   And as under such
diet and exposure the number of sick increased, so was more work thrown
on those who remained".

Hamley then quotes Lord Raglan himself as saying that men were on duty
five nights out of six a large proportion of the time constantly under
fire.   The men had been two months without a change of clothing.   Food
was not the worst problem since the ration of biscuit, salt meat and rum
was generally forthcoming.   But the means of cooking the meat was lacking
and the unvaried diet brought with it scurvy and other diseases.

The front line soldiers, including of course the 41st, were being
deprived of fuel, rice, flour, vegetables and tea which had been landed
at Balaclava but the "Q" branch of the time was not very efficient.

By the end of November, Hamley observes, there were 8,000 in hospital
though many men did not survive the ordeal of the journey there.   He
says: "Lifted from the mud of the hospital tent, and wrapped in their
wet blankets, the sick were placed on horses, a dismal troop;   some with
closed eyes, livid cheeks, little other than mounted corpses;   some
moaning as they went and almost ready in their weariness to relax their
hold of the pommel and bury their troubles in the mire beneath.

"Some fever-stricken, glaring with wide eyes void of speculation, for
whom the passers-by, if they saw them at all in their hurried, insane,
glances, existed only as more of the phantoms that haunted their delirium.

"Bound for the great hospital at Scutari, the ghostly train would toil
on, wading and slipping past the dying horses, the half-buried bullocks,
the skeletons and carcases in various stages of decay and on, always
through deep mire, to the place of embarkation.

"New miseries lay in that word.   Lying amid crowds of other sick
and wounded on the bare planks, in tortured lassitude or lethargy,
without proper food, medicine or attendance, they were launched on
the wintry sea.

"Their covering was scanty, the roll and plunge of the ship were
agony to the fever-strickened and the maimed.   In place of the hush,
the cleanliness, the quiet silent step that should be around the sick,
were sounds such as poets have feigned for the regions of the damned;
groans, screams, entreaties, curses, the straining of the timbers, the
trampling of the crew, the weltering of the waves.   Not infrequently
the machinery of the overladen ship broke down and they lay tossing for
days, a hell upon the waters."

Which was first hand rhetoric for his Victorian armchair audience
but not a patch on the really moving account of the same period given by
Colour Sergeant George William Evernden, the Rifle Brigade, in his diary
(Three Chose War).

The trough had not yet been reached.   Although Lowry's draft had
brought the men fit for duty in the 41st to about 100, but the next
reinforcements did not join until 21st January, 1855.   Meanwhile fever,
diarrhoea and dysentry had commenced, as Lomax put it, to play "dreadful
havoc".   A particular blow fell when the regimental Medical Officer
Surgeon Anderson and his assistant James Lamont both died of low fever.
Assistant Surgeon R.Woodley was obliged to quit on sick leave.   Three
relief surgeons were all struck down and forced to return to England or
Scutari.   The orderlies were similarly affected.

But Lomax was anxious to paint the brighter side of the picture as
well.   1855 was not going to be as bad a year for the 41st Regiment as
its predecessor had been.   On the 18th January Drum-Major Baird received
an ensigny and fifteen men of the Regiment received the newly created
"Distinguished Conduct Medal with gratuity".   In giving their names
Lomax states that his source are Discharge documents.   They were 2,420
Sgt.James Kahir;   2,104 Cpl. William Burghall;   2,698 Cpl.Patrick Hurley;
1,257 Cpl.David Jones;   1,252 Cpl.Henry Targett;   1,374 Pte.William Bryant;
770 Pte.John Creighton;   1,104 Pte.Charles Horner;   2,235 Pte.John Jones;
3,512 Pte.Francis Lynch;   2,425 Pte.Francis Mackay;   2,627 Pte.James
Sheehy;   1,498 Pte.William Tilley;   1,350 Pte.Robert Welsman;   1,600 Pte.
Thomas Williams.

The Regimental Record Book also recorded Sergeant-Major Harris and
Cpl.Ford who seems to have been recommended by Lt.Col.James Eman, now
promoted to command.

Mess-tin cookery had been the order of the day in November and
December but this was obviously inefficient and was dropped in favour of
the re-establishment of cooking by messes early in 1855.   In other
respects the administration of the 41st must have been greatly superior
to that of some other regiments, where it had virtually broken down.
The men, for one thing, were paid regularly by a committee of officers
which had taken over the duties of the paymaster who had fallen sick.
The imprest money for this purpose, strangely, arrived from the Royal
Engineers.

Then follows a passage in Lomax of unusual interest. He says:
"The demand for accountants and clerks for the duties of the division
and for pay sergeants of companies to the regiment, tried the
capabilities of the non-commissioned officers severely.

"Unremitting care and attention had been paid to the education of
the non-commissioned officers prior to the war and Lieut. Cary Barnard
had introduced a system of examination for promotion of non-commissioned
officers to higher grade.

"This system, having been rigidly pursued for five years previous
to the war, had produced a spirit of emulation (competition) which
diffused education throughout the regiment and supplied the unusual
demand caused by death and sickness throughout the campaign".

Pte. Thomas Vincent had been present with the Regiment for more
than those five years and on February 5th, 1855 he was promoted
corporal.

During January the 41st were still guarding the trenches which entailed
a march of two miles each way from their camp. So enfeebled were they,
says Lomax, by dysentry and diarrhoea from the effect of nothing but salt
rations that they found this march very harassing and fatiguing.
Invariably a few men would have to fall out on the way but would rejoin
their companies within half an hour. They were working till they could
no longer walk. They then went into hospital from which the outlet was
death.

Men were relieved after twelve hours duty because of the severity
of the weather. Sheepskin coats (the poshteens of the North West
Frontier of India), long boots and warm clothing of every description
had been issued early in the year, but sickness did not abate and must
have been aggravated by the only shelter available, being tents which
were pitifully inadequate through the severe frosts. But in spite of
the conditions it was almost incredible how high a standard the 41st
managed to attain.

The day after Cpl. Vincent's promotion, a welcome draft of three
officers and 98 men arrived from home. Later in the month Major
General Pennefather resumed command of the 2nd Division and at once
ordered an inspection of the 41st and, evidently confident of what he
would find, invited several other generals along. One of them, whom
Lomax erroneously promoted Lieut.General seven months in advance of that
event, was Sir George Brown.

General Brown passed high praise on the men of the 41st and the
inspection was considered to be proof that organisation and good
discipline still prevailed amongst the regiments in the Crimea.

For the first time, it is possible to state with certainty the
number of Vincent's company. This was No.6 company to which the
officer signing his pay book (now Lieut.) G.Peddie belonged.

By the end of March the regiment had been moved to huts, though the
officers remained under canvas. The improved shelter and better weather
soon reduced sickness. Furthermore fresh rations were beginning to
arrive and the quality of the meat improved. The clothing situation
also became much better. An extra suit of clothing was issued together
with a canvas suit, the forerunner of denims, for wear in the trenches.
None of these items appear as debits in Vincent's pay book so they
appear to have been a free issue.

VII - CLOSING MONTHS OF THE SIEGE

The summer months through to the final fall of Sebastopol, involving
the construction between the French and ourselves of fifty miles of
trenches, involved a form of warfare that in scale, duration and intensity
was only once to be outstripped in the experience of the army. That, of
course, was in W.W.1.

Throughout the period the 41st suffered a steady drain of casualties.
Lomax remarks that it was rare for a night to pass without the parties
holding the trenches suffering casualties.

Captain Rowlands, in a letter, vividly describes this duty. He
wrote:- "On Sunday evening I went into the trenches. The weather which
had been threatening for the previous day or two, burst about eight o'clock
in the evening and lasted, without interruption, until eight on the
following evening.

"I never saw men suffer more; I know I never did. There we were,
paddling about in mud averaging from three to eighteen inches in depth.
It was worse for us because we were in a new portion of the trench made
the previous day within fifty yards of the Russians who had established
rifle pits in front of us.

"They are good marksmen and appear to be always on the look out.
For directly a particle of a body exposes itself, either through a hole
in the gabions, or over the parapets, so certain would a bullet lodge
either in the object aimed at or somewhere near.

"I was so glad when morning dawned, for I had scarcely a firelock that
would go off, so thoroughly were we drenched. If the enemy had come on
we should have been obliged to have depended entirely on our bayonets -
no bad things when properly used".

This letter of Captain Rowlands reveals how unreliable the new Minies were becoming. By a strange paradox, the seasoned regiments such as the 41st did not have the Minie replaced by the new Enfield Rifles until February 1856. On the other hand reinforcements such as the 48th (Northamptonshire Regiment) began to be re-equipped with the Enfield a year earlier while still at Corfu. The 48th did not arrive in the Crimea until 21st April, 1855 forming part of the 2nd Brigade, 4th Division.

All the more odd, therefore, that it was the less well equipped veteran divisions who were chosen for the final assault on the Redan in September.

Meanwhile the allies had been building up their artillery strength and on June 6th opened what was called the third bombardment of Sebastopol with 457 guns, the Russians replying with about the same number.

The allied plan was to construct a series of trenches, creeping ever nearer the main defences of Sebastopol. Only later, when the allied ammunition situation had improved, were orders given for constant and harrassing rifle fire. It was the Russian gunners at their embrasures who suffered most and, being unreplaceable by militiamen, as the Russian infantry were, this led to an increasing number of Russian guns being unmanned.

In the final three months of the siege, there are really two dates that stand our in Cpl. Vincent's record. Indeed, an entry in his pay book leaves one wondering why he was not the recipient of one of the Distinguished Conduct Medals. The entry, signed by Capt. Edmund Harvey reads: "In having served with zeal and distinction in the Trenches and for distinguished active service in the defence of the Quarries 8th June 1855".

In fact it was very nearly the 41st who had to capture the Quarries in the first place. Major General Pennefather, the divisional commander sent for Lt. Col. James Eman, C.B., the C.O. and told him that the 41st had been selected for the assault on the Quarries, the choice being induced by the confidence the general had in the regiment.

However 200 of the regiment were on another duty and the general had to give another regiment the honour. The second choice were not only successful in taking the Quarries, but managed to beat off all Russian counter-attacks in the night.

On June 8th the 41st furnished a large working party to complete the dangerous task of reversing the captured Russian trenches. This was under Captain Rowlands and Lieut. Peddie, respectively commanding the grenadier company and 6 company, which included Vincent. As Lomax says: "Our men were on this occasion as much engaged in keeping the Russians at bay as in forming the parapet, which on commencing the day's work, gave but slight protection to the diggers who suffered many casualties. The exertions of this party were mentioned favourably by Lord Raglan in his despatches. Trench duty from then on was reflected in the increased casualties caused by the shorter distance across No-man's land.

On June 9th there was a $4\frac{1}{2}$ hour armistice to bury the dead. The
men of the 41st thought the disrespect with which the Russians handled
the bodies of their men was terrible.

From February to May Lieut. G.Peddie was Cpl.Vincent's company
commander, but on May 28th Lieut. J.Lockhart arriving with a draft, including
Lieut.W.Johnson and fifty men, took over No.6 Company. In June and July,
Lockhart signed Cpl. Vincent's pay book as a lieut. In August he signed
again, but now as a captain. By September 1st, Lockhart had assumed
command of 5 Company, while command of No.6 reverted to Lieut. Peddie.
It was Peddie who signed his pay book in September and October. The
importance of this is in deciding whether Cpl. Vincent was among the
300 under the C.O. Lt.Col. Eman who stormed the Redan on 8th September or
whether he was one of the 100 men under the second in command Lt.Col.
J.E.Goodwyn who formed the working party in the trenches.

It is almost certain that he was in the trenches because that is
where Lt.Peddie was and, if it comes to that, so was Capt.Lockhart.
Lt. Peddie was, at that time, the only officer with No.6 Company and
presumably he had his own men under his command.

While Lomax does not state very much about George Peddie, except that
he was promoted Captain 26th February, 1856, and died 11th September, 1869,
and was awarded the Order of Mejidie and the Sardinian Medal; he did have
a biography of Lockhart.

As these were the two officers directly associated with Thomas Vincent
in that year of destiny, Lockhart's biography is given. Lomax says:
"James Augustus Lockhart was the son of James Lockhart of Sherfield House,
Hampshire and Lanhams Essex. He carried the Queen's Colour of the 41st
when the regiment landed at Scutari. He was gazetted ensign in the 41st
on 13th May, 1853 and Lieut. 6th June, 1854 and on the 8th September he
was the only fatal casualty in the trench party, which also had three men
wounded.

The 8th September, 1855, the day chosen for the assault on the Redan
was very curious for the reason that, immediately afterwards, the allies
believed they had suffered a reverse, because they failed to capture the
Redan and suffered heavy casualties in that failure. And yet the assault
seems to have been enough to convince the Russians that it was no longer
possible to hold Sebastopol and by 7 o'clock on the 9th September they had
pulled right out of the town.

Major L.L.Gordon states in British Battles and Medals that the Sebastopol
clasp had the qualifying dates 11.9.54 to 11.9.55 although he describes
the Crimean medal as covering the period 28.3.54 yo 30.3.56. There seems
little reason for the final date because an armistice was arranged on
28.2.56 to last till 31.3.56. This was prolonged on 30th March till
further notice but meanwhile the Treaty of Paris was signed on the same date.

By this reckoning, however, those who arrived in the Crimea after 11.9.55 ought to have received the medal without clasp; since there were continued hostilities. Yet they did not. When the family of Cpl. Charles Williams (8th Hussars) tried recently to claim a Crimea medal for their forebear, the Military Secretary wrote to state categorically that Cpl. Williams did not arrive in the Crimea until 28th September 1855 "sometime after the final qualifying date for the award". (See Three Chose War)

So the 8th of September, the eleventh and last of Cpl. Vincent's battles (not to mention the couple of dozens lesser actions) deserves to rate as a very important day indeed. In fact it should rate with Alma, Inkerman, Balaclava and Little Inkerman as the five decisive battles of the Crimea.

The 41st on the 8th were divided into two parties with separate roles. The storming party consisted of 300 men under Lt.Col.Eman and Captain Rowlands and the working party in the trenches of 100 men.

Lieut. Byam, who only arrived in the Crimea on 16th June, in a letter home, gave this version of Col. Eman's orders to the regiment on parade the night before. Col. Eman said: "We are going at the town tomorrow, provided the French take the Malakoff. The detail is as follows:- one hundred men of the Buffs as covering party; one hundred and fifty men of the same to carry the ladders, wool bags etc. One thousand men for the storming party, consisting of five hundred of the Light and five hundred of the 2nd Division, the latter consisting of two hundred of the 62nd and three hundred of the 41st of whom I am one."

The Redan was in the form of a triangle with its apex pointing towards the allies' lines. Its walls were protected by a deep ditch the spoil from which had been thrown up to form a glacis. Any penetration of the apex would meet concentrated fire from the trench dug across the base of the Redan.

The Malakoff was another strong point in the outer defences of the town and the north side of the Karabel Ravine. Its basis was a knoll which the French had to take before the attack on the Redan was to be attempted.

The Malakoff was captured and a Tricolour flew from it at 11.55 on the 8th, the signal for the assault on the Redan which began in two waves. The Light Division storming party led, having won the toss for the honour, to be quickly followed by the 41st with fixed bayonets. The Grenadier Company, led by Captain Rowlands were the first "over the top" as they left the forward trench and surmounted the glacis.

The trench was fairly easily crossed with ladders and by men hauling each other up. The 41st rushed forward into the Redan where they found the storming party of the Light Division in some disorder. All came under heavy fire from "every nook and corner of the Redan". The assailants did their best to return the fire but owing to the method prevalent in 19th Century wars of mixing parties of different regiments, the officers found it difficult to organise a party to rush the Russian trench.

Lt.Col. Eman, perhaps the true hero of Vincent's whole story and obviously a quite exceptional officer, had collected men of the 41st to follow him. He was well inside the Redan when he was shot in the lung. Just before this, Lieuts. Lowry and Byam had passed him with some thirty men. Col. Eman had shouted to them: "That's right, Byam, lead them on, there are more of our men in."

But when the Colonel was shot, it took the impetus out of the charge and men began taking up firing positions until they were counter attacked by a large force of Russians who drove them with the bayonet back into the apex of the Redan.

Captain Every, who had only joined the regiment with a draft two days before, gathered twenty men who rushed in after him. They were shot down at once and Every was killed leading them.

A one-sided fire fight developed between the attackers, who had now become the cornered defenders in the inner apex of the Redan, and the Russian marksmen who had much the better of it.

Occasionally an officer gathered a few men together and attempted a last rush. Capt. Rowlands bore his usual charmed life. Leading one rush a bullet passed through his forage cap, just under the grenade and went through his hair.

Later on in the attack he was again leading the men on, when a Russian threw a grape shot at him which hit him in the eye and knocked him down. No sooner was he up and on his legs than a similar missile hit him in exactly the same place and knocked him down again. Towards the end of the attack both sides were running out of ammunition and threw grape or large stones at their opponents.

There were many acts of bravery by officers and men of the 41st in the abortive attack. Colour Sergt. Fitzgerald was commissioned Ensign for gallantry, but he died two months later at Malta from his wounds. Sgt. O'Neill and Cpl.Starkey received the Legion of Honour. Colour Sergt. Kelley and Privates Garvey and Kenealy the French Medaille Militaire.

There was naturally a post-mortem on the supposed failure at the Redan and the consensus of opinion, according to Lomax, was that the number of troops in the assault was "ridiculously inadequate"; that troops already in the trenches were used instead of passing fresh troops through; that the attack was made on too narrow a front and there was no proper chain of command. All of which seem today to have been proper comments.

In just one and three quarter hours British troops lost 158 officers and 2,026 men killed and wounded. Of these the 41st lost two officers killed and five wounded; with 162 men killed and wounded. That is about fifty per cent of the party engaged.

Early the following morning (Sept.9th) the 41st paraded with the rest of the brigade and marched into Sebastopol. Lomax remarks that the Redan itself "presented a most horrible spectacle; the ditch choked with dead and dying and far inside the work many bodies of the storming party of the 41st were found".

VIII - AFTERMATH

The regiment paraded on the 11th to bury Col. Eman and Capts. Every and Lockhart.

During the rest of the month, although the Russians were still in the field, work was concentrated on preparing winter quarters including a regimental guardroom, cookhouse, tailor's shop and hutting for some of the officers who were still under canvas.

The hospital huts were walled round and everything done in readiness to withstand the winter's cold weather. The ruins of Sebastopol provided much timber for these building operations.

On 29th September the first distribution of the Crimea medal was made. The 41st received 85 which were distributed by the C.O. now Lt.Col. Julius Goodwyn. Lomax, who mentions this, makes no comment on the number, nor does Whitehorne writing 32 years later. It seems likely however that these medals all had the clasps Alma and Inkerman, unnamed as issued and 85 probably represents the number of officers and men still serving with the battalion who were entitled to the two bars, of course including Vincent. The clasp for Sebastopol had yet to be authorised and was also awarded to Thomas Vincent.

Two drafts of reinforcements reached the regiment in September. That on the 6th, already mentioned and commanded by Capt. Every, was in time for the fighting at the Redan, but the second draft, consisting of one officer, two sergeants and 11 privates, like Cpl. Charles Williams of the 8th Hussars had nothing but an entry in their pay books to show for it afterwards.

On 15th November there was a very serious explosion in the allied lines in an English magazine. It occurred in the afternoon when shot and shell and grape-shot fell among the huts of the 2nd Division nearly a mile away. Fortunately for the regiment most of the 41st were out road building and the only casualty was Bandsman Latty of Cpl. Vincent's company who was killed by a shell bursting in his hut.

The Light Division were not so lucky, suffering 79 killed and wounded.

The winter was a mild one and many of the men were recruits badly in need of training. Not surprisingly some of the veterans were promoted among them Cpl. Thomas Vincent who was promoted Sgt. on December 11th, 1855

It should be noted that as Lomax says:- "a dilatory (sometimes lively) fire was kept up by the enemy on the town they had so obstinately defended but there were very few casualties."

During the rest of the winter there was little to report except that a nation now conscious of the miseries of 1854/55 had seen to it that there was proper clothing. Lomax says that in comparison with its predecessor "the winter of 1855-56 was one of indescribable comfort".

Bt. Major G.Page, who joined on December 6th became Sgt. Vincent's company officer and from April to July it was Capt. Harvey. Captain and Adjutant James Hamilton signed Vincent's pay book in March 1856.

Another event reflected in Sgt. Vincent's pay book was a grand review of the English Army on the 17th April, 1856, when 30,000 British troops were on parade and the Russian, French and Sardinian generals honoured (Lomax' word) the parade with their presence. The Russians, after all were still enemies less than three weeks before.

In that month's entry in the pay book Sgt. Vincent took "1 Tunick 1 pr. Cloth Trousers and 2 pairs of boots". (One to grease and one to polish perhaps).

On 17th June, 1856 the 41st and six companies of their old comrades the 49th embarked on H.M. Steam Transport "Transit" reaching Spithead on 26th July.

In the London Gazette of 16th October, 1855, authorisation had been given for three more battle honours to be carried on the Colours of the 41st "Alma, Inkerman and Sebastopol" bringing to six the total of battle honours to which Sgt. Vincent had made his personal contribution.

Sgt. Vincent was a natural survivor. Before the assault on the Redan, Sir William Russell the famous correspondent of The Times had remarked that the veteran divisions averaged only 15 old soldiers in each battalion.

The 41st lost 13 officers during the war. Six were killed in action; four died of wounds and three died of disease. 13 officers were wounded. 110 n.c.o's and men were killed in action, 426 were wounded and 246 were invalided. 277 men died of disease.

These figures are taken from Lomax who adds that the strength of the battalion when it landed at Scutari on April 15th, 1854 was 863 and a further 521 reinforcements arrived prior to 9th September, 1855.

Although Sgt. Vincent came through, he is of course numbered among these statistics as one of the wounded at Inkerman.

On arrival in England the 41st went by rail to Aldershot and the next day July 29th they were inspected by Queen Victoria who referred to "her high sense of the gallantry they displayed before the enemy, as well as admiration of the fortitude with which they supported the hardhips incidental to the late campaign".

On the following day she returned accompanied by members of the English and Russian Royal families.

And four days later as a mark of gratitude for seventeen years faithful service Sgt. Vincent was reduced to the rank of private. The presumption must be that there was no longer a Sergeant's vacancy.

This may have been connected with orders for the Regiment to hold itself in readiness to proceed to Dublin. It did not however go there, but on August 4th proceeded by rail to Dover.

On 3rd October 28 men were discharged as being "unfit for service". Pte. Vincent was not one of them. In the spring of 1857 the 41st proceeded by detachments to various stations in the West Indies.

Thomas Vincent did not go with them. He left the colours in February 1857 with a total of 17 years and 7 months service.

On March 24th, 1857 he was admitted an Out-Pensioner of the Royal Hospital, Chelsea and granted a pension of 1/- (5p) a day. This was increased to 1/3d (just over 6p) a day on the 28th August 1866 by which time he was 44 years of age. His Out-Pensioners number was 16,020.

In conclusion it seems right to say that while Thomas Vinxent may not have been an outstanding man, nevertheless he was clearly one of those whose solid worth forms the backbone of any regiment.

A postscript may not be inappropriate. It concerns Captain D.A.N.Loma himself, whose brilliant chronicle of his regiment's story stands as a model of such work after 80 years. A year after he produced the history, in a limited edition of 250 copies, he was killed in action at the Battle of Driefontein, South Africa, March 10th, 1900.

Whitehorne recalls the scene. "He was shot at two yards range as he was cheering on the line into the trenches with the words "Welch now is your chance. Come on boys, follow me. Charge. Come on the good old Welch". It was an echo of Col. James Eman at the Redan.

Soldier's Name and Description.

1110 Thomas Vincent

Enlisted for the *14th* Regiment of *Foot* on the *19th July 1839* at *Bristol* . in the County of *Summerset* at the age of *18* years *4* months. Born in the Parish of *Chalcot* in or near the Town of *Bath* in the County of *Summerset*

Trade or Calling, *Smith*

Last Permanent Residence, *Bath*

Size *5* Feet *5¾* Inches.

Complexion *Fresh* Eyes *Gray* Hair *Dark Brown*

Marks *Nil*

Services (if any) prior to his Enlistment into *the 14th Reg*

None

A Soldier is not to marry without a written sanction, obtained from his Commanding Officer. Should he marry without this sanction, his Wife will not be allowed in Barracks, nor to follow the Regiment, nor will she participate in the indulgences granted to the Wives of other Soldiers.

Soldier's Number.

Every Soldier is to communicate to his Friends the number by which he is known in the Regiment, and to acquaint them, that in all inquiries which they make after him, whether addressed to the Regiment or to the War Office, they are to state such number.

Soldier's Signature.

Whenever a Soldier who cannot write makes his Mark in acknowledgment of having received Pay or Allowances, &c., such Mark is to be witnessed.

Amount of Bounty received by the Soldier in Cash	£	
Ditto in necessaries	£	
Total Bounty . .	£	

The necesssaries to be provided out of the Soldier's Bounty are specified in Her Majesty's Clothing Warrants, and the said necessaries are subsequently to be kept in a due state of repair, or when become unserviceable by fair wear, or when lost or injured through the Soldier's own neglect, are to be replaced by Stoppages from his Pay.

Services Abroad.

East Indies, Cinde & Affghanistan
Landed in England 3rd July /43 for Malta 28th
March /54 In Turkey 15th Apr. 1854
In Crimea 14th Septr /54 G.W.V.

Promotions or Reductions in Rank.

Promoted to Corpl. 1st February 1855
To Serjt 11th December 1855
Reduced 3rd August 1856
G.W.V.

If Married, Date and Place of Marriage, and Christian name of Wife.

17 Octr 1852 at Sligo
Mary G.W.V.

Children (if any) date and place of Birth and Christian name.

One Girl   47145

Wounds.

Wounded in the _____ '54 at the battle
of Inkerman in the left instep
      E. Sadleir Lieut.

Distinguished himself.

Received a Medal for service in Affghanistan
present in Action with the Enemy 1st June & 28th
April 29 May 30 August 5th & 29th Sept besides
several minor affairs in and between the Pishan
and Kyber battles

Present in the Action at Alma 20th of September 1854 —
Sortie on the 26th of October; Inkerman on
the 5th November; and at the assault on the
Redan Sebastopol 8th of September 1855
In having served with zeal & distinction in the trenches
& for distinguished active service in the defence of the Quarries
8th June 1855 —
Medal & 3 Clasps for _____ Edmund Harvey Lieut in Regt.

Status Censu...	Year 1855		
	Amount due to Soldier	Amount due from Soldier	Officer's Signature to Credit to Debit.
January			
February	13		
March			
April			
May			
June			
July			
August			
September			
October			
November			
December			

Amount of Clothing	Date when received by the Soldier.	Signature of the Soldier

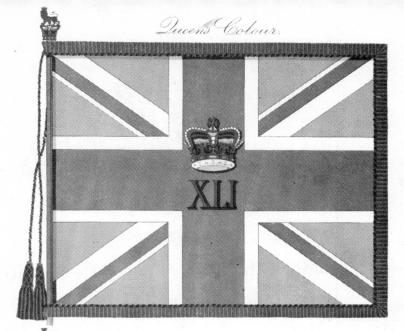

Regimental Colour.

Presented at Sheffield, 1862.

No. 2.

N° 17 - B 28.8.66   *Increased from 1/- to 1/3*

Service.
Years.   Months.

17 - 7

Stature.
Feet   Inches

5 - 5½

Hair.
Brown

Eyes.
Hazel

Age.
At this time.

44

THIS is to Certify, that *Thomas Vincent* late of the _____ *41st* _____ Regiment of Foot, was admitted an **OUT-PENSIONER** of Her Majesty's Royal Hospital at Chelsea, on the _____ *24th March* _____ 186*7*, and receives a Pension of _____ *1/3* _____ per Diem.

Given under my Hand, this *28th* **day of** *August* **186***6*.

George Hutt

Secretary and Registrar,
Royal Hospital, Chelsea.

N.B.—Where good grounds exist for preferring an application on any subject connected with Pension, the letter should be addressed to "The Secretary, Royal Hospital, Chelsea, S.W.:" the applicant must state distinctly his name in full, his Regiment, rate of Pension, and date of admission to Pension—quoting, at the same time, the following Number *16,020*

G [6,??] 5000 3 66